Constitutional Law
as Fiction

L. H. LaRue

Constitutional Law as Fiction

Narrative in the Rhetoric of Authority

The Pennsylvania State University Press
University Park, Pennsylvania

Library of Congress Cataloging-in-Publication Data

LaRue, Lewis H.
     Constitutional law as fiction : narrative in the rhetoric of
authority / L. H. LaRue.
          p.   cm.
     Includes bibliographical references and index.
     ISBN 0-271-01406-7 (cloth : acid-free paper)
     ISBN 0-271-01407-5 (pbk. : acid-free paper)
     1. United States—Constitutional law—Fiction.   2. Judicial
opinions—United States—Methodology.   3. Rhetoric.   I. Title.
KF4552.L37   1995
342.73—dc20
[347.302]   94-15750
                                                                  CIP

Copyright © 1995 The Pennsylvania State University
All rights reserved
Printed in the United States of America
Published by The Pennsylvania State University Press,
University Park, PA 16802-1003

It is the policy of The Pennsylvania State University Press to use acid-free
paper for the first printing of all clothbound books. Publications on uncoated
stock satisfy the minimum requirements of American National Standard for
Information Sciences—Permanence of Paper for Printed Library Materials,
ANSI Z39.48–1984.

To
James Boyd White
mentor and friend

Contents

Preface

A preface is the place where one engages in shop talk and thanks one's friends, and since this book is about my research into constitutional law as a branch of rhetoric, I want to thank those who taught me to rethink constitutional law, rhetoric, and the connection between the two. I had a lot of rethinking to do, since I was taught at Harvard by masters of the orthodox school—among them, Paul Bator, Paul Freund, and Henry Hart—that constitutional law was a subdivision of analysis, not rhetoric. They were magnificent teachers, and I count it as one of my good fortunes to have been taught by them. Having seen analysis so splendidly executed, it has been a daunting task for me to replace analysis with rhetoric.

My reeducation began at the Civil Rights Division of the Justice Department. I thank especially my mentors in the department, J. Harold Flannery and D. Robert Owens, who taught me back in 1965 what it was to practice constitutional law. And for insight into the human reality of constitutional law, I owe the most to the good citizens of Mississippi, both black and white, who taught me what was at stake. By the time that those in the department and in Mississippi had finished with me, I knew enough to know that something was wrong with what I had learned at Harvard.

When I began teaching, my immediate task was to rethink the subject, and I was lucky enough to receive aid and comfort over the years from a fine group of friends. For help in understanding history, I owe the most to Eugene Genovese, Wythe Holt, and Calvin Woodard. For leading me toward the inner secrets of constitutional argument, I am indebted to Paul

Brest, Lief Carter, Jan Deutsch, Sanford Levinson, Jeff Powell, and Mark Tushnet. But it was not enough to know the history and structure of constitutional argument; I needed to understand more about alternative forms of argument. Milner Ball, Tom Shaffer, and Joseph Vining taught me how to see the connections between law and theology. Judy Koeffler, Teresa Phelps, Peter Teachout, Jim White, and Mary White taught me about the connections between law and the humanities, especially literature.

I would like to thank several people who helped me bring this book to completion: Philip Winsor, my editor, guided me gently through the process; Allan Ides, my colleague in the teaching of constitutional law, read the penultimate draft and led me toward clarity in several obscure places; and Andrew Lewis, my copyeditor, carved away some of the fat and errors. And of course, neither these three, nor any of those listed in the previous paragraph, should be blamed for the many defects that remain.

This book is dedicated to one of my mentors and friends, James Boyd White. Many years ago, I taught his book, *The Legal Imagination*, and it was both an inspiration and a revelation. We corresponded, we met, we became good friends. Over the years, we have reviewed each other's manuscripts, and I have learned much from that process, both from reviewing his drafts and from reading his reviews of mine. This one is for friendship.

Introduction

The title of this book, *Constitutional Law as Fiction*, will suggest different things to different readers. Those within the law-school community might expect a connection with that rather loosely defined group of studies called "law and literature."[1] Those in the larger academic community might anticipate that this book is part of the revival of "rhetorical studies."[2] And finally, that mythical beast, the common reader, who is happily innocent of trends in academia, might suspect a joke, since to suggest that constitutional law is a branch of fiction might strike such a reader as a comic claim.

I address these expectations as follows (anyone who wishes may jump ahead to Chapter 1 and will probably miss little): This book is not a comedy for one very good reason: I am a typically dull academic. Were I as talented as

---

1. Someone who wishes to know more about the enterprise of "law and literature" should examine two recently published journals, *Cardozo Studies in Law and Literature* and *Yale Journal of Law and the Humanities*. For a bibliography, see James Elkins, "A Bibliography of Narrative," 40 *J. Leg. Ed.* 203 (1990).

2. Someone who wishes to know more about the classical tradition of the study of rhetoric should consult Brian Vickers, *In Defense of Rhetoric* (Oxford: Clarendon Press, 1988), which is a highly biased polemic that also happens to be quite scholarly. For the modern and nontraditional study of rhetoric, see the twenty-two essays gathered in *The Rhetoric of the Human Sciences*, ed. J. Nelson, A. Megill, and D. McCloskey (Madison: University of Wisconsin Press, 1987). And I cannot resist citing Arthur Quinn, *Figures of Speech* (Salt Lake City: Gibbs M. Smith, 1982), which is a profoundly witty book.

John Cleese, I would write a comedy about law as fiction, but I'm not, so I won't.

To explain how this book differs from studies we classify under the heading "law and literature" is slightly more complicated. Indeed, I participate in the enterprise known as "law and literature." I teach a course inspired by the work my colleagues in this field have done, and I have written some book reviews and articles on the topic. However, this particular book cuts through the law at a slightly different angle. As my title, *Constitutional Law as Fiction*, suggests, I will examine the "fictions" that appear in judicial opinions and try to explain how these fictions make the opinions persuasive. My focus differs, consequently, from that of those who tend to focus on literature and use insights drawn from there to reflect on the law.[3] I am not reading literary fictions to gain insight into law; I am reading law as itself an example of literary fiction. By the way, I have no objection to the general project of using fiction to generate insight into law; I do it myself, although I do not believe that literature is a uniquely privileged route to moral insight. And at any rate, this book is not about that. Another trend among scholars is to call for narrative within the project of jurisprudence itself, the claim that abstract theory has weaknesses that narrative can rectify.[4] Perhaps, but I think that narrative's ability to cure theory depends on the particular narrative and the particular theory. But at any rate, this book is not about that either. I am not trying to bring narrative into jurisprudence; I wish to critique the narratives that are already there.

This book is part of the study of rhetoric in human affairs. As I have already stated, I contend that judicial opinions contain fictions and that these fictions make the opinions persuasive. Since rhetoric is the study of persuasive speech and writing, it follows that rhetoric is the category into which my book should be pigeonholed. Our Western tradition of rhetoric goes back to the Greeks, as most Western traditions do. A thumbnail history of rhetoric in our Western tradition would highlight Greek originality, Roman adaptations, transformations (due to the loss of texts) in the Middle Ages, the Renaissance revival, and the discrediting of rhetoric that accom-

---

3. For a recent example of this genre, see Richard Weisberg, *Poethics and Other Strategies of Law and Literature* (New York: Columbia University Press, 1992). I state my differences from Weisberg in "The Problem of Theory in *Poethics*" 15 *Cardozo L. Rev.* 1093 (1994).
4. Perhaps the most prominent exemplar of this trend is Patricia J. Williams, *The Alchemy of Race and Rights* (Cambridge: Harvard University Press, 1991). For a general discussion, see the Symposium of Legal Storytelling, 87 *Mich. L. Rev.* 2073–2494 (1989).

panied the early modern age in the seventeenth and eighteenth centuries.[5] The twentieth century has seen rhetoric's revival, and anyone foolish enough to use "rhetoric" as a keyword in a computer search of a library catalog will be overwhelmed with the number of responses. Furthermore, if one tries to sample the enormous number of books that mention rhetoric in their title, subtitle, or table of contents, one will quickly discover that these books do not have much in common. When the great Roman teacher Quintilian wrote his massive treatise on rhetoric, he spoke from within a unified tradition, to which, it is rather apparent, we moderns have no counterpart.[6] Consequently, when I say that this book is part of an imagined body of scholarship that I might call law and rhetoric, I have not said much. There is no handy consensus about what a book of "law and rhetoric" should be.[7]

The word "rhetoric" goes back to a Greek verb that means "to speak" and is derived from the same root as the words "verb," "irony," and "word." Very early in the tradition, rhetoric became the study of persuasive speech, not speech in general, and it has been quite routinely extended to the study of persuasive writing as well as persuasive speech. Unfortunately, this root meaning of the word is not enough to ground a common discipline, since speech and writing can persuade in many different ways and at many different levels of conscious and unconscious operation. For example, in this book I wish to pursue such theses as the following: the authors of judicial opinions intend to persuade the reader that the result reached is right; these opinions contain fictions; the use of fiction is essential for persuasion. None of these is obscure or esoteric, but there is no established consensus on how to investigate them or on the terms with which investigation should proceed.

Since there is no well-established convention for investigating judicial

---

5. See Vickers, *In Defense of Rhetoric.*

6. For some of the crucial evidence on the scope of the modern revival of rhetoric, see Richard A. Lanham, *A Handlist of Rhetorical Terms*, 2d ed. (Berkeley and Los Angeles: University of California Press, 1991). Lanham notes in the preface to the second edition (ix–xi) that he had originally imagined that his Handlist would be useful to graduate students of English, but that the audience has been far broader than that. "It has also been found useful by scholars working in strands afar remote from literature—art history and anthropology, economics and philosophy" (ix). One who wishes to get a sense of the range and diversity of this phenomenon should consult Lanham's own recent reflections on the matter (cited in his Handlist at x and 203).

7. An attempt to define the field by way of example is James Boyd White, *Justice as Translation: An Essay in Cultural and Legal Criticism* (Chicago: University of Chicago Press, 1990), but he has not persuaded such reviewers as Mark Tushnet, "Translation as Argument," 32 *Wm. & Mary L. Rev.* 105 (1990), or Sanford Levinson, "Conversing about Justice," 100 *Yale L. J.* 1855 (1991), which is unfortunate.

rhetoric, I choose to introduce my inquiry by placing it in a historical context. The modern university can trace back to the medieval period many of its institutional forms. However, the curriculum of the medieval university differed markedly from that which prevails today. Then as today, the university had a basic liberal arts division and its graduate departments, and the medieval graduate departments of law, medicine, and theology survive in modern universities, augmented by a vast profusion of other graduate programs. The additions of new departments at the graduate level constitute a rather minor change in structure, but the fundamental reworking of the liberal arts has been truly radical. In the medieval university, the liberal arts were structured into a lower division and a higher division; the lower-level courses were logic, grammar, and rhetoric; the upper-level courses, arithmetic, geometry, astronomy, and music.[8] The names of the seven courses have survived, but the overall structure has not. In the modern university, logic is now in the philosophy department, grammar is now in the linguistics department, and rhetoric is dispersed throughout the humanities and social science departments, although there are departments in some universities which have the word "rhetoric" in the department name.

From my point of view, what is most significant about the modern scene is the dispersion of the study of rhetoric versus the concentration of the study of logic and grammar. This institutional fragmentation reflects a larger intellectual diffusion, namely, that the logicians and linguists have a central theory to follow or contest, whereas rhetoricians do not. For logic, 1879 is the key year. In that year, Gottlob Frege published his *Begriffschrift (Conceptual Notation)*, which revolutionalized the study of logic.[9] (In fact, the impact of Frege's ideas was delayed until 1910, when Whitehead and Russell published their *Principia Mathematica*, which consolidated the revolution that Frege had unleashed.)

In linguistics, 1957 is the key year. In that year Chomsky published his *Syntactic Structures*. To be sure, Chomsky's work has been controversial; furthermore, his project has itself gone through several stages of develop-

---

8. For a general introduction, and a translation of one of the basic texts, see William Harris Stahl, with Richard Johnson and E. L. Burge, *Martianus Capella and the Seven Liberal Arts*, 2 vols. (New York: Columbia University Press, 1971 and 1977).

9. See Terrell Ward Bynum, *Conceptual Notation* (Oxford: Clarendon Press, 1972), for a translation of the *Begriffschrift*. This book includes a useful introduction; however, I recommend instead Gregory McCulloch's book *The Game of the Name* (Oxford: Clarendon Press, 1989), which does the best job of showing how fundamental Frege's logical theories are to modern philosophy. Of course, one is free to disapprove of modern philosophy, but that is a different issue.

ment, so that his recent work differs markedly from his early work. Nevertheless, we can say that although the majority of linguists differ sharply with Chomsky on numerous issues, he has defined the field.[10]

In rhetoric, there has been no comparable event. Kenneth Burke, perhaps, comes closest to having defined the field, but his books A *Grammar of Motives* (1945) and A *Rhetoric of Motives* (1950) do not stand in the same relationship to the field of persuasive language as *Begriffschrift* and *Syntactic Structures* do to their fields. The problem for rhetoric is that persuasive language is not a unified object in the way that the human capacities to reason and to speak are. All humans learn to speak in such a rapid and miraculous way that linguists postulate a grammatical capacity that is part of the innate biological endowment of the species. And similarly, the capacity to reason and count seems innate, although our sophisticated modern technologies of logic and mathematics certainly do not. Persuasion is complicated, messy, and diverse; it—apparently—lacks a unified structure analogous to those on which logic and grammar seem to rest. At any rate, no one has demonstrated such a structure yet.

Consider, for example, the distinction that Chomsky makes in linguistics between "external language" and "internal language." His thesis is that linguistics should study the internal representation, the internal knowledge, that speakers have of their language, not the external phenomenon.[11] Many critics have assumed that Chomsky has this backward, but his position makes good theoretical sense, in that the biological endowment that makes us capable of speaking is the right sort of theoretical object, namely, it is uniform across the species. On the other hand, the rich phenomenon of language spoken in a community is too rich to be the sort of uniform object about which one can generalize theoretically. By analogy, the same can be said of persuasion. When one speaker attempts to persuade another, the complex second-guessing that each makes about the other's knowledge and motives, their relative positions of power, the constraints put on them by the political and economic context, and so forth, make generalization difficult and problematic.

Socrates makes an analogous argument in Plato's *Phaedrus*. In this dialogue, Plato has Socrates tell Phaedrus that it does no good to say that a

---

10. For a map of the debate, see Rudolf P. Botha, *Challenging Chomsky* (Oxford: Basil Blackwell, 1989), which is a rather mean-spirited, but useful, compendium. A recent set of essays, *The Chomskyan Turn*, ed. Asa Kasher (Oxford: Basil Blackwell, 1991), contains a general account by Chomsky, "Linguistics and Adjacent Fields: A Personal View."

11. See Noam Chomsky, *Knowledge of Language* (New York: Praeger, 1986), 15–40.

speech should have a beginning, a middle, and an end, or that a speech could be sublime or common in its diction, or rapid or deliberate in its delivery. All such generalizations are of no value unless one knows when and how to use them, which in turn requires one to know the conditions of the human soul and how and why the soul can be moved. In the following passage, Socrates states his program for investigating rhetoric:

> The function of speech is to influence the soul. It follows that the would-be speaker must know how many types of souls there are. The number is finite, and they account for the variety of individual characters. When these have been determined one must enumerate the various types of speech, a finite number also. For such and such a reason a certain type of person can be easily persuaded to adopt a certain course of action by a certain type of speech, whereas for an equally valid reason a different type cannot. When the student has an adequate theoretical knowledge of these types, the next requisite is that his powers of observation should be keen enough to follow them up when he comes across them in actual life; otherwise he will be no better off for all the instruction received in the lecture room. When he is not only qualified to say what type of man is influenced by what type of speech, but is able also to single out a particular individual and make clear to himself that there he has actually before him a specific example of a type of character which he has heard described, and that this is what he must say and this is how he must say it if he wants to influence his hearer in this particular way—when, I say, he has grasped all of this, and knows besides when to speak and when to refrain, and can distinguish when to employ and when to eschew the various rhetorical devices of conciseness and pathos and exaggeration and so on that he has learned, then and not till then can he be said to have perfectly mastered his art.[12]

In the passage quoted, Socrates states a cogent agenda, but one which we may not be able to fulfill. An enumeration of the different types of souls and knowledge of why different rhetorical devices work differently for each are still beyond us. At best, we can look at certain rhetorical devices (in my case the story, the narrative fiction) and ask why it might persuade a particu-

---

12. Plato, *Phaedrus*, trans. Walter Hamilton (London: Penguin Classics, 1973), 91–92.

lar group of people (in my case, lawyers and judges). Like Chomsky, Socrates tells us that we may not rest content with investigating the speeches that have been made within the community; we must go further and investigate the human psyche. Until we are able to do so, certain preliminary investigations are in order; this book is merely one of the many preliminary investigations that are possible.

Let me now set out the road map for this book. In Chapter 1, I explain what I mean when I state that judicial opinions contain fictions. Chapters 2 and 3 are both about Chief Justice John Marshall, who is without doubt the most important figure in American constitutional law. The fictions I investigate are important because John Marshall exploited them. I have selected two stories made famous by John Marshall: the story of limits, namely, that constitutional rights are not subject to legislative whim and that the Constitution sets limits that are above politics, and the story of growth, namely, that the Constitution is a living, dynamic institution that grows to meet contemporary needs. The tensions—or to be blunt, the inconsistencies—between these two stories intersect most dramatically when dealing with cases involving race and the equal protection clause. Does the equal protection clause limit the power of government to make distinctions on the basis of race? Or does it empower government to act to change the racial inequalities that exist among us? The answer is "Well, sort of both, but then . . . ," which means that we have a problem. In Chapter 4, I try to show something about the nature of this problem. Finally, in Chapter 5, I tell a story about evaluating stories.

1

Telling Stories

The title of this book, *Constitutional Law as Fiction*, summarizes my thesis, which is that the proud towers of the law are built not on the level bedrock of "fact" but on the perplexed terrain of "fiction," that judicial opinions are filled with "stories" that purport to be "factual" but that instead are "fictional," and furthermore, that these "fictions" could not be eliminated without crippling the legal enterprise. (By the way, I acknowledge the ambiguity of "fact," "fiction," and "story," but in due course hope to explain what I mean by these words.)

I

My claim that legal discourse is made of stories that are "fictional" will strike many as curious, since legal discourse does not obviously resemble the short story or the novel. For example, a judicial opinion customarily cites other cases that seem to be relevant precedents. Novels and short stories do not usually start by citing precedents. The practices of "stating an issue" or "citing a rule" are also central to legal argument, but rarely found in novels or short stories. Indeed, the average judicial opinion follows a standard format that differs sharply from that used by novelists.

Consider, for example, the typical opinion in a court such as the Supreme Court of the United States. It usually begins with the procedural history (a summary of what has happened in the trial court and the intermediate appellate court) and an event history (a summary of the out-of-court facts, namely, the events that generated the case or suit). The order in which these two summaries are presented may vary, but they customarily come at the beginning of the opinion. I can illustrate this common pattern by quoting from *Everson v. Board of Education*,[1] which I shall return to later in order to illustrate the thesis of "law as fiction." The opinion begins as follows, with events first, procedure second:

MR. JUSTICE BLACK delivered the opinion of the Court.

A New Jersey statute authorizes its local school districts to make rules and contracts for the transportation of children to and from schools. The appellee, a township board of education, acting pursuant to this statute, authorized reimbursement to parents of money expended by them for the bus transportation of their children on regular busses operated by the public transportation system. Part of this money was for the payment of transportation of some children in the community to Catholic parochial schools. These church schools give their students, in addition to secular education, regular religious instruction conforming to the religious tenets and modes of worship of the Catholic Faith. The superintendent of these schools is a Catholic priest.

The appellant, in his capacity as a district taxpayer, filed suit in a state court challenging the right of the Board to reimburse parents of parochial school students. He contended that the statute and the resolution passed pursuant to it [by the school board] violated both the State and the Federal Constitutions. That court held that the legislature was without power to authorize such payment under the state constitution. 132 N.J.L. 98, 39 A.2d 75. The New Jersey Court

1. 330 U.S. 1 (1947).

of Errors and Appeals reversed, holding that neither the statute nor the resolution passed pursuant to it was in conflict with the State constitution or the provisions of the Federal Constitution in issue. 133 N.J.L. 350, 44A.2d 333. The case is here on appeal under 28 U.S.C. § 344(a) (*Everson*, 3–4)

It is also customary for the author of a judicial opinion to state at the beginning of the opinion a summary of the issue presented for decision. Once again, I shall use Justice Black and *Everson* as an illustration:

The only contention here is that the state statute and the resolution, insofar as they authorized reimbursement to parents of children attending parochial schools, violate the Federal Constitution in these two respects, which to some extent overlap. *First.* They authorize the State to take by taxation the private property of some and bestow it upon others, to be used for their own private purposes. This, it is alleged, violates the due process clause of the Fourteenth Amendment. *Second.* The statute and the resolution forced inhabitants to pay taxes to help support and maintain schools which are dedicated to, and which regularly teach, the Catholic Faith. This is alleged to be a use of state power to support church schools contrary to the prohibition of the First Amendment which the Fourteenth Amendment made applicable to the states. (5)

In short, judicial opinions do not look like fiction, their authors do not believe that they are writing fiction, and their readers (other judges, lawyers, law professors, and law students) do not normally imagine that they are reading fiction. Instead of describing their work as writing fiction, most judges would say that deciding cases is their primary responsibility. People bring their disputes to court, and if they are unable to negotiate settlements, they submit their disputes to a judge (or, a judge and jury). As one goes up the judicial ladder, the focus on deciding cases remains, but an additional function—declaring and clarifying the law—becomes important. When we get to the United States Supreme Court, in a case like *Everson*, which I have just cited, the responsibility of declaring law becomes primary. (In this book, I limit myself to discussing Supreme Court opinions.)

Those who declare law have an awesome responsibility, especially when they must declare constitutional law. We expect of them, and they expect of themselves, caution, care, and meticulous attention to detail. Look back at the two paragraphs I have quoted from *Everson;* the procedural and event histories are short and incomplete, but also quite specific and concrete in the details. This quality of meticulous care is normally present in other parts of the standard judicial opinion: precedents are cited, and quoted from, with care to get the page numbers right; the "issue" is stated in a pedantic, almost fussy, manner; and in general, the prose of the opinion is normally perceived as dense and technical. (Hugo Black's prose differs from that of most judges by being far more colloquial than is customary, and so Black does not illustrate all of my generalizations.) However, I wish to argue that one should not be misled by judicial prose into believing that constitutional law is a technical enterprise. Instead, I suggest that one should listen for that moment in legal discourse when a story is told. These moments are crucial.

Judicial opinions must be persuasive if the enterprise of judge-made law is to have the power that it has. Lawyers and judges need to believe in what they do. The spirit and self-confidence of the judiciary rests on their belief in the rectitude of their enterprise. Since persuasion is so important, my metaphor "law as fiction" is apt. Without persuasion, law could not be law, and without fiction, there would be no persuasion.

I hope that the above establishes the topic. If so, let me now state two qualifications on the scope of my inquiry and on how I understand my thesis, "law as fiction." First, the phrase "law as fiction" is intended as a description, and describing law as fiction is merely one of many ways to describe law. For example, we can describe law as a process for settling disputes, or as a way of organizing power, or as an expression of the underlying social structure of our society. In this book, I shall not examine the merits (which are many) of these alternative descriptions; instead, I shall try to explain my own.

However, it is surely worthwhile to pause and consider a problem of descriptions. There is a fundamental error here that must be avoided: one must avoid the superstition that any one description will necessarily or logically exclude any other. If I describe a man as tall and heavy, I should not be understood as denying that he is graceful and quick. So too, if I describe law as the way those with power have organized and coordinated their power over the rest of us, I should not be understood as denying that law is also a necessary technique for resolving disputes. Both descriptions can be true. To be sure, if I say that a man is tall, I have excluded the possibility that he is short. Furthermore, even though a tall man can weigh less than a short man, the odds are that he will not. Thus, the description of a man as tall does not exclude the description of that man as light, but it does make it less likely. Similarly, two different descriptions of law could be logically compatible, but unlikely.

How, then, should a reader understand my claim that we can describe law as fiction? Are there other descriptions with which it is logically inconsistent? And are there descriptions with which mine *could* coexist, but is not likely to? The thesis of "law as fiction" can coexist with other theses such as "law as power" or "law as violence," as the late Robert Cover has argued.[2] For example, one might say that the stories told conceal the violence of the law or somehow enable the law's actors to do violence with a good conscience. However, I do not try to work out any such links in this book; instead, I limit myself to the fictions that are told. Even within these limits, and allowing for the possibility of multiple, alternative descriptions of law, my thesis (that judicial opinions contain fictions that are absolutely essential to the business of judging) is inconsistent with one fairly common analysis of judging, which goes somewhat as follows: those who judge start with rules which they derive from their reading of cases and statutes; but the rules standing alone are not sufficient; in order to use rules wisely, judges must consider the purposes behind the rules, namely, the principles and policies that make the rules appropriate and rational. (Giving a citation here is almost foolish, since one could easily assemble a book-length bibliography on the many variations of this standard thesis; so I will limit myself to the book from which I was taught.)[3] The standard thesis reflects the obvious, that judges do talk about rules and purposes, about principles and policies, but errs in asserting that this rationalistic account of judging subsumes the necessary and sufficient conditions of judging. I assert that stories are necessary.

Second, not only is the phase "law as fiction" just one out of many possible descriptions, it is also merely a description, and not an evaluation. I know that many people consider the word "fiction" pejorative; fact is good and fiction is bad. But I think that the truth is more complicated than that. (I will not take the high ground and argue that Shakespeare and Sophocles tell more truths than those who purport to be factual; they do, of course;

---

2. See Robert M. Cover, "Violence and the Word," 95 *Yale L. J.* 1601 (1986); "Nomos and Narrative," 97 *Harv. L. Rev.* 4 (1983); and the bibliography of his work, 96 *Yale L. J.* 1725 (1987). One might say that Cover spent most of his all too short career puzzling over the links between law, violence, and stories.

3. Henry M. Hart Jr. and Albert M. Sacks, *The Legal Process: Basic Problems in the Making and Application of Law* (Cambridge, Mass.: multilithed, 1958). I was taught this book, in a course by the same name, by Professor Hart in my second year of law school.

but my thesis is far more pedestrian, and so I shall proceed on a lower level of discourse.) The complexity of good and bad in fiction arises from the tangled meaning of this curious word. In this book, I use the word "fiction" in the same way that it is used in common speech, but with a twist. Let us start with ordinary usage. As I understand our everyday speech, a fiction is a story about something that didn't really happen. The *American Heritage Dictionary of the English Language* puts it more formally: "A literary work whose content is produced by the imagination and is not necessarily based on fact."

Ordinary usage—which I have described informally as a story about something that didn't really happen—is necessarily the place to start, but it would be disastrous to leave it at that. Consider my dictionary's statement that a fiction "is produced by the imagination and is not necessarily based on fact." This dictionary definition is unsatisfactory because it implies (without clearly stating) a sharp dichotomy between two kinds of stories: those produced by the imagination and not necessarily based on fact, *versus* those not produced by the imagination and necessarily based on fact. However, this dichotomy may not exist. Can we produce stories without using the imagination? And is it possible to have stories that are based solely on the facts? If not, then almost all discourse is "fictional"; or if I may put this thesis more cautiously, most discourse is in part fictional. Consider, for example, history. Historians write accounts "based on fact," but good historical accounts are also "produced by the imagination." When historians try to explain the course of events, they must compare the several different explanations that are possible, and they must try to say why one explanation fits the facts better than another. But where do the explanations come from? The majority of historians do nothing more than struggle with the explanations that their predecessors have bequeathed to them. We honor as great, however, those who extend our knowledge by the strength of their imagination. We honor those whose explanations are new, challenging, and enlightening. (American historians who exemplify this trait include Frederic Jackson Turner, whose frontier thesis revolutionized the study of American history, and Francis Parkman, whose vast imaginative powers enabled him to create an exceptionally vivid account of the French and Indian wars.) Furthermore, the imagination is not limited to proposing hypotheses, which the facts then adjudicate. Would that life could be so simple. The witnesses who wrote the documents that historians use may have been biased, so that one must cross-examine these documents carefully, and one must have a good imagination before one can ask good questions. Even after we have accepted certain documents as trustworthy, they may be ambiguous or incomplete on crucial issues. But one cannot be sensitive to ambiguities or absences without imagination, and furthermore, resolving ambiguities and restoring absences are creative, imaginative acts.

If all accounts have fictions that cannot be removed, then fact and fiction are not dichotomies. Every story will have some of both. Our honorable ambition may be to present facts, but human limitations will frustrate us; we will never tell a story that is not fictional in part. If this be true, if fact and fiction are necessarily intertwined, then it follows that the word "fiction" should not be a pejorative. If fiction is necessary, then it is idle to condemn it.

However, not all stories are equal. Some are better than others. As we examine the stories that judges tell, we find here too that some are good, some are bad. Judges tell us these stories to persuade us that the path of the law should run one way, not another, and we may be persuaded on some occasions but not on others. Furthermore, the ratio of fact to fiction in a story does not correspond to the ratio of truth to falsehood in it. After all, we can never know facts with certainty; we are limited to probabilities. As every lawyer knows, eyewitnesses can be mistaken, and there is a margin of error in laboratory tests. In short, the facts in a story are never simply true; rather, they must be considered more—or less—likely. Moreover, even if our facts are probable, they may be incomplete, and thus misleading. For example, suppose it to be highly probable that a worker who was fired gave speeches that the boss despised. This short statement is necessarily incomplete. Suppose further that this worker fought with coworkers at the workplace, and note how that fact changes the possible stories. In other words, an incomplete set of facts, even if all of the details are true to a high degree of probability, will suggest to us a story that is likely to be false. And conversely, just as a mass of facts need not guarantee a true story, imagination need not generate falsity. A story only marginally supported by the facts and largely generated by the imagination may yet be true. In the simplest case, imagination can make a lucky guess, which later investigation corroborates. In more complex cases, a discerning imagination may be our only guide to truth. Further investigation may be impossible because the evidence is lost; witnesses may have died; records may have been lost; physical traces may have deteriorated. And if the key facts concern human intention— whether an act was malicious, or merely thoughtless—then imagination may be the only possible guide into the workings of the human psyche.

In the above, I have used the word "story" without defining it; I have suggested that a story can be true even though largely fictional, but I have not clarified how I am using the word "story." Fortunately, to use so casually a key word like story is harmless, since legal stories are far less complex than novels, plays, or narrative poems. Judges do not write like Joyce or Borges. Consequently, I think it best to keep the analysis as simple as possible, and I shall do so by accepting a straightforward definition that the novelist Reynolds Price has asserted. In his discussion of biblical narratives, Price states:

> From Genesis we gather that Adam . . . invented narrative; when God hunts out the human pair after their fall, Adam says, "I heard Your voice in the garden and feared, since I'm naked, and hid myself"—a chronologically consecutive account of more than one past event, with attention to cause and self-defense: thus a narrative.[4]

Price's elegant summary works for legal stories, all of which attend to chronology, causation, and evaluation. For purposes of this book, nothing more complicated is needed.

The foregoing constitutes the abstract part of this introduction; let me now be more concrete. To illustrate the presence of fiction in the law, I discuss a few of the key cases governing the church-state relationship. I start with an attempt to show that the legal discourse about law and religion includes stories along with other more familiar topics. The familiar topics in the field of law and religion include legal dissection of the leading precedents, philosophical puzzles about the difficulty of defining religion, sociological analysis about the place of religion in American life, political judgment about whether religion divides or unites us, and historical discussions about how things have changed or not changed. The discourse on any of these themes can be broadly theoretical or intensely empirical; but whether theoretical or empirical, a funny thing seems to happen along the way to the conclusion. No matter how a discourse starts, sooner or later the analyst slips into the narrative mode. (For instance, even in the writings of Immanuel Kant narrative is "inserted into that blank place where the presumed purely conceptual language of philosophy fails or is missing."[5] And if an abstract thinker like Kant must use narrative, then everyone must.)

4. Reynolds Price, A Palpable God: Thirty Stories Translated from the Bible: With an Essay on the Origins and Life of Narrative (New York: Atheneum, 1978), 8.
5. J. Hillis Miller, The Ethics of Reading: Kant, de Man, Eliot, Trollope, James and Benjamin (New York, Columbia University Press, 1987), 24.

Are these stories mere illustrative embellishments? Or are they the deep structure of cognition on which the theory rests as mere superstructure? My own hunch is that the latter is true, although this assertion is not easily proved or disproved. Instead, let us turn to the legal discourse on law and religion and listen to the stories that are told.

II

The leading case, the case that is the foundation for establishment-clause jurisprudence, is the well-known *Everson v. Board of Education*, from which I have already quoted. I wish to analyze the story told in *Everson*, but let me start by reviewing some of the undisputed facts of that case. Plaintiff was a taxpayer who sued to contest expenditures of a New Jersey school board. The board had acted under a New Jersey statute that authorized it to provide transportation for students; the statute gave the board discretion to provide transportation either by buying its own buses, by making contracts with carriers, or by reimbursing parents. The school board chose to reimburse. A statute that provides in general terms for the transportation of children to school is, of course, unremarkable. Furthermore, there is nothing especially remarkable about the board's having discretion to choose among several different ways of providing transportation. The novel twist of the New Jersey statute, and this is the fact that generated the litigation, is that the statute authorized the school board to provide transportation for those who were attending private schools as well as those who went to public schools.[6] Acting under this statute, the school board reimbursed parents for the cost of transportation to Roman Catholic parochial schools. It is this expenditure that is the disputed act in the *Everson* case.

6. "Whenever in any district there are children living remote from any schoolhouse, the board of education of the district may make rules and contracts for the transportation of such children to and from school, including the transportation of school children to and from school other than a public school, except such school as is operated for profit in whole or in part.

"When any school district provides any transportation for public school children to and from school, transportation from any point in such established school route to any other point in such established school route shall be supplied to school children residing in such school district in going to and from school other than a public school, except such school as is operated for profit in whole or in part." *New Jersey Laws* (1941), c. 191, p. 581; *N.J.R.S. Cum. Supp.*, tit. 18, c. 14, § 8. The statute can be read as requiring, and not merely authorizing, school boards to provide transportation to children attending private schools, although this issue of statutory construction is not a part of the case.

Justice Black wrote the opinion for the majority, which held that the school board's actions were constitutional. There were four dissenters, and Justices Jackson and Rutledge wrote dissenting opinions. I do not wish to spend any time on a legal analysis of the several opinions, but I would like to say that the judges do not differ substantially among themselves on the legal issues. Everyone agreed that the First Amendment—"Congress shall make no law respecting an establishment of religion"—by virtue of the Fourteenth Amendment, also restrained state government. Furthermore, the majority and the dissenters agree more than they disagree on how to interpret the prohibition. The test that Justice Black propounds is as follows:

> Neither a state nor the Federal Government can set up a church. Neither can pass laws which aid one religion, aid all religions, or prefer one religion over another. Neither can force nor influence a person to go to or to remain away from church against his will or force him to profess a belief or disbelief in any religion. No person can be punished for entertaining or professing religious beliefs or disbeliefs, for church attendance or non-attendance. No tax in any amount, large or small, can be levied to support any religious activities or institutions, whatever they may be called, or whatever form they may adopt to teach or practice religion. Neither a state nor the Federal Government can, openly or secretly, participate in the affairs of any religious organization or group and *vice versa*. In the words of Jefferson, the clause against establishment of religion by law was intended to erect a "wall of separation between church and State." (*Everson*, 15–16)

This test was not itself objectionable to the dissenters; their complaint was that the majority had not in fact applied its own test.[7] Whether the majority or the dissenters are right on the only question that divides them—the proper application of an agreed-upon test—is an interesting matter, but it is not my subject. Instead, I wish to turn to the stories that the several judges published. Interestingly enough, the several narratives are not inconsistent; Justices Black, Jackson, and Rutledge seem to agree on certain fundamental

---

7. As Justice Jackson put it, "In fact, the undertones of the opinion, advocating complete and uncompromising separation of church from state, seem utterly discordant with its conclusion yielding support for their commingling in educational matters. The case which irresistibly comes to mind as the most fitting precedent is that of Julia who, according to Byron's reports, 'whispering "I will ne'er consent"—consented.'" *Everson*, 19.

"narrative tropes" to tell the story about the establishment clause. Black's story is more economical; as a result, it is the one commonly reprinted in case books, and the one I shall discuss.

Recall that Black began his opinion with a short statement of the school board's decision to reimburse parents for the cost of transporting their children to parochial schools. He then described the litigation that followed and identified the issues raised by this litigation. The due process issues were dismissed in a mere three pages (*Everson*, 5–8). Counsel had argued that the school board violated the due process clause by giving public money to private persons. But Black responded that education was a public purpose and that government was privileged to carry out public purposes by giving money to private persons who would in turn spend it on the public purpose. He stated: "Subsidies and loans to individuals such as farmers and homeowners, and to privately owned transportation systems, as well as many other kinds of businesses, have been commonplace practices in our state and national history" (7).

Having disposed of the due process issue, he then turned to the prohibition against establishing religion. Black's discussion of the religion clause began with neither legal analysis nor any discussion of precedents. Instead, he noted that those who adopted the clause had a clearer idea of the evils they intended to prohibit than do the current generation of Americans, who have, indeed, to the degree that the prohibition has been effective, forgotten the evils to be prohibited. As Black put it:

> The New Jersey statute is challenged as a "law respecting an establishment of religion." The First Amendment, as made applicable to the states by the Fourteenth, *Murdock v. Pennsylvania*, 319 U.S. 105, commands that a state "shall make no law respecting an establishment of religion, or prohibiting the free exercise thereof. . . ." These words of the First Amendment reflected in the minds of early Americans a vivid mental picture of conditions and practices which they fervently wished to stamp out in order to preserve liberty for themselves and for their posterity. Doubtless their goal has not been entirely reached; but so far has the Nation moved toward it that the expression "law respecting an establishment of religion," probably does not so vividly remind present-day Americans of the evils, fears, and political problems that caused that expression to be written into our Bill of Rights. Whether this New Jersey law is one respecting an "establishment of religion" requires an understanding of the meaning

of that language, particularly with respect to the imposition of taxes. Once again, therefore, it is not inappropriate briefly to review the background and environment of the period in which that constitutional language was fashioned and adopted. (8)

Black asserts that we need the history of the prohibition in order to understand it; he presents a narrative that comprises eight pages in the United States report and leads up to his test for judging, which I have already quoted. Black clearly believes that his narrative explains and justifies the test, and he further believes that his narrative is good, factual history.

Justice Black's story professes to be about "the background and environment of the period in which that constitutional language [the establishment clause] was fashioned and adopted." He begins his story by writing: "A large proportion of the early settlers of this country came here from Europe to escape the bondage of laws which compelled them to support and attend government-favored churches." Let me pause over this first sentence, since some careful attention to it will let me justify my use of the word "fiction." I suggest that Justice Black's sentence, in which he asserts that a large proportion of the early settlers came to escape the bondage of religious establishments, is not the sort of sentence that can be "based on fact," since there can be no evidence that will either prove or disprove it. We have no evidence, and so we do not know, why a "large proportion of the early settlers" came to this country. We do know something about the *types* of reasons they had for leaving Europe. Some came to make a fortune, some came to escape poverty, some came for adventure, some came to flee criminal or civil prosecutions, some came to escape the failure of their lives in the old country, and some came indeed as Black says, "to escape the bondage" of religious oppression. For most of those who came, we have no evidence about why they came. For an insignificantly small number, we have letters and diaries, but a scrupulous historian would be cautious about making inferences from such evidence. A letter justifying and explaining the trip to someone back in the old country may not be the best evidence for actual motives. Furthermore, diaries must be carefully interpreted, since diaries are sometimes, but not always, written to describe an ideal self rather than an actual historical self. For all of these reasons, we can say that Black's opening sentence is fictional.

Some of the facts in Justice Black's story can be shown to be more or less true—or false—to some degree of probability. We can test for truth such assertions as how many (rough estimate) settlers came, when (what year or decade) they came, where (general area) they settled, and so forth. Some of these facts cannot be accurately known; lacking an accurate census, for example, we might have to estimate the number of settlers to the nearest thousand. Uncertainty in interpreting the settlers' motives, however, is a more radical form of uncertainty. Why did the colonists come to America? This is a question that they themselves might not have been able to answer. (We are often unable to answer such questions about ourselves. Why did I go to law school? Why did I fall in love with, and marry, the woman who is my wife? I can't answer these questions.) And if they could not, then we cannot, and this inability to answer has nothing to do with our lack of information about them. To be sure, if we had more information we could better interpret their motives, but we can never know them. Given the uncertainty of our interpretations, we might simply forgo interpreting. Some historians are purists about interpretation, refusing on grounds of principle to speculate about human motives and other psychological states. However, the human tendency is to interpret, and there is nothing wrong with the attempt. In everyday life and in courtrooms, we fill in gaps in our evidence, we build bridges between facts in order to interpret human conduct. Black has offered an interpretation, and this alone is no vice. Even so, we can be skeptical; we can recognize what he has done; we can say that he has constructed a fiction to support his interpretation; we can ask whether there might be better interpretations that could be offered.

Since we have here a fiction, we might classify it as an example of the narrative trope known as "the quest." As one reads, the Book of Exodus seems to hover in the background. In the Exodus version of questing stories the storyteller describes the evil being fled from, and Justice Black obliges us. He describes the European experience from which the "early settlers" have fled as "filled with turmoil, civil strife, and persecutions, generated in large part by established sects determined to maintain their absolute political and religious supremacy" (8–9). This description of the "Egypt" from which the settlers were fleeing is the sort of description a lawyer might call the truth but not the whole truth. Consider for example the qualifying phrase "in large part." If the "turmoil, civil strife and persecutions" were caused "in large part" by religious strife, then it follows, at the very least, that such calamities were not caused *solely* by the religious, acting for religious reasons. The larger truth would be that motives were mixed, and that both the religious and the nonreligious acted for reasons of lust, greed, power, and envy, as well as for theological and religious reasons. I suspect that it is beyond our power to discern the mix of motivations, and furthermore, I doubt our ability to generalize over the many different cases of "turmoil, civil strife, and persecutions." Different persecutions have different causes. In short, Black's quasi-statistical "in large part" is unjustified.

Since what we are reading is a fiction, and not a bare factual recital, we should be cautious and alert and question its basic rhetorical tropes. As a story, what sort of world does it imagine? In this world, how does causation operate? In this imagined world, what are the fundamental values that people hold dear? How are these values threatened, and how are they defended? As I interpret the story, it seems to me that the fundamental values in this world are the values of freedom and peace, that freedom and peace are threatened by turmoil and persecution, and that religion (or religious establishment) is the chief cause of these threats. (Note that I have put the phrase "or religious establishment" in parentheses. A careful examination of Black's rhetoric shows that he shifts back and forth from talking about "religion" and about "a religious establishment." Read narrowly, he is talking about the dangers and threats of an establishment; but the overtones of the rhetoric make it sound as though he is talking about religion itself.)

This story of religion as the chief threat to peace is an important one, and part of its importance lies in the identity of the storyteller. Hugo Black is one of the great rhetoricians among those who have published in the United States Reports, and being one of the greats, he impels us with the power of his prose; he does not deign to argue; he tells powerful stories. Part of the power of his rhetoric flows from his integrity and authenticity as a jurist; he obviously believes his story; we have here no dissembling, no cleverness, no display for the sake of display. And part of the power comes from his skill with the English language; his prose is vivid, clear, and rapid. The combination of character and eloquence is overwhelming. Every year, students and teachers reread this story. Every year, students and teachers, myself included, are swept up by the power of Black's prose. Let me quote another excerpt—also from *Everson v. Board of Education*—that shows Black at his most powerful and most convincing.

Catholics had persecuted Protestants, Protestants had persecuted Catholics, Protestant sects had persecuted other Protestant sects, Catholics of one shade of belief had persecuted Catholics of another shade of belief, and all of these had from time to time persecuted Jews. (9)

This part of the story is overwhelming, and it would be a hopeless task to argue against it. To be sure, it is merely the truth and not the whole truth, but such qualifications seem weak and captious in the face of such powerful rhetoric. The more complete truth is that persecuting seems natural to humans; religion can provide reasons for persecution, and if religion is absent, other reasons will be found. One might note that few centuries have equaled our own in slaughter, and that our charnel houses have been run by secular murderers as well as pious ones. The right and the left have proved to be equally adept at slaughter, be they godless or devout. Black surely knew these facts, but the generative force of his story is to associate persecution with religion, and the association is made so indelibly that religion appears to be one of the worst calamities let forth upon our globe. If this be religion, surely anyone who loves freedom and peace must be ever on guard against the destruction that it can set loose among us.

The fiction about persecution differs from the one about motives. When we attribute motives to others, we fill in the gaps in the evidence by imagining a story. The fiction about persecution works differently; this fiction selects out from the collective slaughters one subset of them, the religious persecutions, and builds a story out of the subset; it imposes order by selection. This process of ordering by selecting is legitimate, of course, since it is necessary. Just as we must attribute motives to others and to ourselves, so too must we select the relevant facts and ignore the irrelevant, or else we will be disabled from thinking about our world in an orderly fashion. Black is interpreting those clauses in the First Amendment that mention religion, and so there is no wrong in focusing on the subset of religious persecutions, even though this may distort the dynamics of persecution, and even though it oversimplifies the mixed motives present in religious persecution. Complete accuracy in a matter such as this is impossible.

Let me continue with Black's story. As stated above, the story begins with the "early settlers" fleeing the "bondage" and the "persecutions" that characterized the European experience. But in Black's story, as in any good story, there are some twists and turns; one cannot leap too quickly to the part where they lived happily ever after. Like the ancient Israelites fleeing from Egypt, the "early settlers" must suffer in the desert. As Black puts it:

> These practices of the old world were transplanted to and began to thrive in the soil of the new America. The very charters granted by the English Crown to the individuals and companies designated to make the laws . . . authorized these individuals and companies to

erect religious establishments which all, whether believers or non-believers, would be required to support and attend. (9)

In other words, they sought a new Garden of Eden, but the serpent had stowed away in the cargo hold. This part of the story is rather less powerful than what has gone before, since it tends to be droll. First, the word "transplant" is a curious metaphor; to say that the "practices" were "transplanted" suggests that practices are objects, like plants, and that these objects are separate from the human beings who use the fruit of the tree. (The fruit here is poisonous.) If the practice is a separate object, then the transplant metaphor is apt; if not, it is not. An alternative account might say more bluntly that the experience of the New World was the same as that of the Old. Indeed, to blame the mean old Brits for sneaking religious establishments into the charters relieves the colonials from most of the blame, which is rather comical. This droll story removes from consideration the possibility that the colonials were not fleeing *from* religious bondage; they were fleeing *with* it.

At any rate, the serpent, once let loose in the new America, beguiled the settlers, and the New World witnessed a "repetition of many of the old-world practices and persecutions" (10). In describing this "repetition," Black echoes his earlier rhetoric:

> Catholics found themselves hounded and proscribed because of their faith; Quakers who followed their conscience went to jail; Baptists were peculiarly obnoxious to certain dominant Protestant sects; men and women of varied faiths who happened to be in a minority in a particular locality were persecuted because they steadfastly persisted in worshipping God only as their own consciences dictated. (10)

However, this story has a happy ending, because it has a hero—the freedom-loving colonials. Since the "early settlers" have been absolved of responsibility (the blame lies in "practices" which have been snuck into the charters), Black is able to portray them as the victims of (or bystanders to) these practices and not the oppressors. Consequently, these victims (or bystanders) can be aroused to change things. As Black puts it:

> These practices became so commonplace as to shock the freedom-loving colonials into a feeling of abhorrence. The imposition of taxes

to pay ministers' salaries and to build and maintain churches and church property aroused their indignation. (11)

As we all know, righteous indignation is a powerful force, and so the "freedom-loving colonials" acted to throw off the yoke of religious establishment.

In order to round off this part of the story, one must give the "how" of the liberation. The culminating point, the terminus ad quem of the story, is the adoption of the First Amendment, which contains the establishment clause that Black wishes to construe. The question is, How do we get to that point? Black notes that many contributed. He writes, "No one locality and no one group throughout the Colonies can rightly be given entire credit" (11). However, as he tells the story, Justice Black makes it clear that he believes that the "one locality" that is most important was Virginia and that the "one group" that deserves the most credit was a group of two, Jefferson and Madison. To be sure, any story will oversimplify complex historical dynamics, but this particular simplification is breathtaking.

Let me summarize, without quotation, the gist of Black's story: The conflict in Virginia came to a head in 1785 when the Legislature took up a bill to renew the tax levy in support of the established church; Madison wrote the Memorial and Remonstrance in protest; in face of public support for Madison, the Assembly postponed consideration of the bill; at the next session, the bill died in committee; the Assembly then passed Thomas Jefferson's Virginia Bill for Religious Liberty. Later, during the drafting of the First Amendment, Madison and Jefferson also played a leading role (11–13).

As a story, this is not merely incomplete, it is implausible, and thus, the worst sort of fiction. The story of religious persecution from which the settlers fled, which I have already discussed, is far more powerful. To be sure, that part of the story is seriously incomplete, and the judgments in it about causation are simplistic; nevertheless, its central core is powerful indeed. The central core of this part of the story is far less powerful. Its basic logic is that those who opposed the Virginia bill to renew the tax levy did so because they were persuaded by the arguments in Madison's Memorial and Remonstrance. If this is so, then the events leading up to the Virginia Bill for Religious Liberty differ from every other event in the history of our species. Surely the more plausible account would begin by supposing that Madison's Memorial and Remonstrance was a symbolic call around which different groups were able to rally for different sorts of reasons. Presumably, each read into the document some of their own ideas, and each must have understood its words partly according to their own predispositions. The key words in the last two sentences are "surely" and "presumably." By these words, I have signaled that we know certain general matters about human affairs; we know that in politics different groups will generally read different meanings into documents such as Madison's. Knowing this, we ought to conduct an undogmatic empirical investigation to ascertain the details of the divergent readings. We would also know that this investigation could never be complete because of gaps in the evidence, that the narrative report of this empirical investigation would inevitably contain some fictions.

For example, were we to conduct an empirical investigation into the events in Virginia, we might discover that a large number of opponents to the tax levy were against it because they were against taxes, not merely taxes for establishment, but any taxes. (Taxes were payable in either cash or tobacco, and the dissenting groups such as Baptists and Presbyterians were short of both commodities.) Other opponents might object to establishment for religious reasons, to protect religion from the corruption by government, and not for the secular reasons that Madison advanced.[8] Furthermore, we might note that Madison and Jefferson were exemplars of the Enlightenment *philosophes* in America and that the number of such *philosophes* in Virginia was rather small. In any historical investigation, one must proceed on the basis of certain assumptions about human motivation, human understanding, and human action before one can even pose questions to be investigated, before one can even know what counts as evidence. The assumption that I am making is that leaders, such as Madison and Jefferson, and followers, such as the people of Virginia, understand issues differently. Indeed, this difference is one of the things that makes leaders leaders. Furthermore, the mass of followers in this case was made up of distinct and differing groups; Virginia in the late eighteenth century was not a homogeneous society. Differing groups understand differently, and of course, these differences are what make them, in fact, different.

Is there anything wrong with Black's story? As I have already said, I hope to use the word "fiction" as a description, not an evaluation. In evaluating Black's story, we can start with the observation that it "is not necessarily based on fact," but then, most stories aren't. A story is told to lend meaning to events, and it is simplistic indeed to suppose that meanings can be straight-

8. Mark De Wolfe Howe, *The Garden and the Wilderness: Religion and Government in American Constitutional History* (Chicago: University of Chicago Press, 1965). When the scene switches to the U.S. Congress, some of those who voted to disable Congress from establishing religion did so to protect state establishments. They were not against establishment; they were against a *national* establishment. Robert L. Cord, *Separation of Church and State: Historical Fact and Current Fiction* (New York: Lambeth Press, 1982).

forward. Most events have more than one meaning, all simultaneously both
partially true and partially false. I don't think we can criticize Black for
telling a story that contains fiction. Even when we recognize that Black's
history is also fiction, we still have not made a very profound criticism. A
modern proponent of Black's story could say the following: a judge must
interpret the text of the Constitution, which entails that he must assign
meaning to it. The only way to assign meaning to it is to put it into a
context, and that entails assigning a particular interpretation (or meaning)
to the context. To do this, one must tell a story that will be in part fictional.
This defense of Black seems quite sound to me. At law, we of necessity
claim that certain events have meaning—guilty or not guilty, liable or not
liable, constitutional or unconstitutional, and so forth. We cannot make
these declarations without telling stories about the contested events. And
when the matter being contested is a text such as the Constitution, a text
that was the product of a human struggle to which the participants assigned
meanings, it is also necessary that we tell stories that assign meaning to the
struggle and the text. However, not all stories are equal; some are better
than others. Furthermore, I am painfully aware that I cannot produce a
better story than Black's. I am an amateur in both history and narratives;
my views have both the strength and the weakness of my amateur status.
Even so, I have some hunches about why Black's story is bad. I cannot
better it, but I know why I reject it.

Justice Black's story is bad because it denies respect to the religious, even
though most of the voters who supported Madison were religious, and con-
fines respectability to the views of elite actors such as Madison. In this story,
religion threatens to produce disorder and persecution, and an established
church seems to be one of the worst calamities ever loosed upon a suffering
humanity; however, the *philosophe* Madison offers peace through enlight-
ened argument and persuasion.[9] As a picture of the world, it seems markedly
undemocratic; as politics in our own polity, it seems to be as dangerous to
the peace as the views that it condemns.

I agree that religion has loosed great horrors on the world; the persecutions
that Black vividly describes are examples. However, religion has also nur-
tured much that is good; our own civil rights movement is an example.
Religion, like secularism, generates both good and bad, and it seems silly
to ask a quantitative question about which side predominates; we have no

9. Let me offer a speculative digression. In cases involving the establishment clause, religion
is seen as a threat, as something to be feared. In cases involving the free-exercise clause, religion
is viewed with sentimental indulgence, as something too weak to protect itself. In neither sort of

technique for counting. Furthermore, there were religious believers who supported the establishment clause; I think that any interpretation of the establishment clause that denies all value to their interpretation is bad. Consider the following story, which is no worse a fiction than Black's story. The religious supporters of the prohibitions against establishment believed, as did many in the late eighteenth century, that our experiment in self-government would fail unless public virtue was widespread among the citizenry, and they further believed that religion was a prerequisite to public virtue. However, they also believed that religion rested on belief and conviction, and that coerced belief was no belief at all. Furthermore, they thought that any government subsidy would lead inevitably to government control of religion, the power of the purse being inevitably the power to regulate, and that governmental control of religion would inevitably corrupt religion, and thus destroy the public virtue that was needed. This pretty story that I have just told may be overdrawn, but it is based on the research of good scholars.[10] Moreover, I agree with the political judgment of Thomas E. Buckley on this topic. Once it was clear that the Episcopal Church could no longer be the sole established church, the legislature had two options, a scheme of multiple establishments, or no establishment at all. Was there to be a general assessment, taxing each for the church of his choice, or was there to be no assessment at all? The Baptists and the Presbyterians came out against the proposal for the general assessment, and they provided the key votes in the struggle. Buckley is surely right when he states: "Had the evangelicals, and particularly the Presbyterians, opted for the assessment bill, Virginia would have had a multiple establishment of religion instead of Jefferson's Bill."[11] If Buckley is right that "the evangelicals, and particularly the Presbyterians," deserve most of the credit, then shouldn't they be central to the story, not Madison? And shouldn't their views be more important than Madison's?

III

Hugo Black has given us a powerful narrative about the events of the eighteenth century. However, we also need a narrative about the modern events

case is religion something to which ordinary standards apply; there is either a special quarantine or a special indulgence.

10. See Samuel W. Calhoun, "Conviction without Imposition: A Response to Professor Greenwalt," 9 *J. of Law & Religion* 289, 293–98 (1992), for a short summary, with citation.

11. Thomas E. Buckley, *Church and State in Revolutionary Virginia* at 175 (Charlottesville: University Press of Virginia, 1977).

that generated the case. Black's opinion is rather skimpy on this issue, and I suspect that one explains this skimpiness by noting that he was writing a majority opinion, which sustained the constitutionality of what the school board did, and consequently, there might have been an incentive to produce a bland and abstract description of the modern events. Black, generally a clear writer, may have avoided characterizing the events in order to preserve a consensus.

However, Justice Jackson, who dissented, did tell a story about the events of modern times, and part of the reason for doing so is that his reading of the facts of the case differed sharply from Black's. Black wrote as though the issue was one of extending aid to private schools as well as public schools, and it just so happened to be the case (an accident of geography, perhaps) that the particular private schools before the Court were also religious schools. This reading of the facts was a crucial step in Justice Black's argument; it permitted him to characterize the reimbursement for transportation as a "public welfare" action (*Everson*, 16–18). Justice Jackson read the record differently. He asserted that the issue was extending aid to Roman Catholic parochial schools and only to Roman Catholic parochial schools. These divergent readings are generated from an ambiguity in the evidence; the school board's resolution is worded in a way that permits either inference, so let me explain this ambiguity.[12] The school board, as noted above, was empowered by the statute to provide transportation to pupils of both public and private schools. In this case, the board exercised its power by passing a resolution, and in doing so, it stated that reimbursement would be provided to pupils attending public schools or Catholic schools within the district. If this statement is an exhaustive description of all of the schools that happened to be in the school district, that is, if the only schools in the district were public or Catholic, then Justice Black has read the facts correctly. However, if there were other private schools in the township, and the school board has excluded them, then Justice Jackson has read the facts correctly. (Obviously, none of the judges thought it was worthwhile to send the case back to clarify the issue, and a modern reader might wonder why. My own hypothesis is that stories are so powerful they can distract one from such technical scruples.)

Given that there are two possible readings, one might ask which reading is more accurate. However, that does not interest me. What interests me is that Jackson's reading led him to tell a story about modern events, not ancient events. In Jackson's story, the religious have set up religious schools to "indoctrinate." Of course, in one sense of the word "indoctrinate," this

12. The text of the resolution is set out in Justice Rutledge's dissent at *Everson*, 62 n. 59; see also 30 n. 7.

assertion is surely true, but what follows from this assertion? Do we imagine indoctrination to be something bad that is also inconsistent with everything that is good? Or is indoctrination something that is respectable? Isn't it true that the public schools "indoctrinate" children?[13] Does Justice Jackson think that indoctrination is something that only bad people do? Unfortunately, the overtones of Jackson's story (although not the explicit statement) are chilling; as Jackson tells the story, the Roman Catholics are engaged in something fundamentally un-American.

He begins as follows:

> It is no exaggeration to say that the whole historic conflict in temporal policy between the Catholic Church and non-Catholics comes to a focus in their respective school policies. The Roman Catholic Church, counseled by experience in many ages and many lands and with all sorts and conditions of men, takes what, from the viewpoint of its own progress and the success of its mission, is a wise estimate of the importance of education to religion. It does not leave the individual to pick up religion by chance. It relies on early and indelible indoctrination in the faith and order of the Church by the word and example of persons consecrated to the task. (*Everson*, 23)

One can read this as flattery since Jackson says that the Roman Catholic Church is acting on the basis of "experience" and that those who run it have made a "wise estimate" of the situation that they face. However, the flattery is hardly complimentary, since the contrast between "pick[ing] up religion by chance" and "early and indelible indoctrination" is a contrast of polar extremes, both of which many people might find threatening. If those are the choices, many would fear to choose, and more important, would not trust those who might chose consistently, without regret, and cold-bloodedly. In Justice Jackson's fiction, the Roman Catholic Church is able to choose, whereas others cannot.

Jackson goes on as follows:

> Our public school, if not a product of Protestantism, at least is more consistent with it than with the Catholic culture and scheme of values. It is a relatively recent development dating from about 1840. It is organized on the premise that secular education can be isolated

13. In *Wisconsin v. Yoder*, 406 U.S. 205 (1972), Chief Justice Burger accepted the Amish plaintiffs' characterization that public high school "tends to emphasize intellectual and scientific accomplishments, self-distinction, competitiveness, worldly success, and social life with other students"

from all religious teaching so that the school can inculcate all needed temporal knowledge and also maintain a strict and lofty neutrality as to religion. The assumption is that after the individual has been instructed in worldly wisdom he will be better fitted to choose his religion. Whether such a disjunction is possible, and if possible whether it is wise, are questions I need not try to answer. (23–24)

In this paragraph the contrast of the preceding paragraph is carried forward; choice is now posed as the opposite of indoctrination, whereas before the contrast was between indoctrination and chance. Furthermore, new themes are added to this rhetoric. It is now asserted that the "culture and values" of Catholicism are inconsistent with the culture and values that are shared by both the public school and Protestantism. It follows that to the extent that the nation is primarily Protestant and is also committed to the public school, then to that extent the nation is founded on principles inconsistent with the "culture and values" of Catholicism. Moreover, if a "strict and lofty neutrality as to religion" is a fundamental thesis of the establishment clause, then the culture and values of Catholicism are inconsistent with the culture and values of the Constitution.

Let me quote one more final paragraph from Jackson:

I should be surprised if any Catholic would deny that the parochial school is a vital, if not the most vital, part of the Roman Catholic Church. If put to the choice, that venerable institution, I should expect, would forego its whole service for mature persons before it would give up education of the young, and it would be a wise choice. Its growth and cohesion, discipline and loyalty, spring from its schools. Catholic education is the rock on which the whole structure rests, and to render tax aid to its Church school is indistinguishable to me from rendering the same aid to the Church itself. (24)

In terms of the story that Jackson has told, the conclusion is inevitable. Having defined the relation between schooling and religion as he has, it follows most surely that to aid the school is to establish the religion. How should we respond to this story? I dislike it, not because it is a story, but because it is a bad story. Jackson is not merely filling the gaps or selectively

---

(211) and thus threatened to inculcate non-Amish values in the plaintiffs' schoolchildren. When I teach *Yoder,* I ask my students whether Chief Justice Burger's description of high school is true or false; they have uniformly told me that his description is true.

emphasizing certain facts; he is contradicting the facts and anathematizing a group. There are at least three inaccuracies. First, his assertion that those who established the public schools intended to "maintain a strict and lofty neutrality as to religion," is not true.[14] Second, he does not acknowledge that Roman Catholics established parochial schools in the United States as a purely defensive measure against the hostile Protestantism of the public schools.[15] And finally, even assuming his account of the Catholics' motives to be true, Jackson is surely wrong in supposing that the Catholic schools in fact execute the purpose he supposes they have. One might suppose that it was the fantasy of certain clerics to have the sort of power that Jackson declares to be the reality. However, the evidence does not support the fantasy.[16]

Although the story is false, it is also a bad story for other reasons. Jackson's story is objectionable because it declares that those among us who wish to set up religious schools are doing so to further a culture and values that are at odds with the fundamental values of the nation. To tell this sort of story is to rest the decision on a vision of what is American and un-American, rather than on an understanding of what is constitutional and unconstitutional. Jackson declares a creed of what is American, and yet he also denounces credal politics.[17] This story purports to praise a "lofty neutrality," yet declares foreign and dangerous the "culture and values" of a large group of citizens. It praises neutrality, but enacts partisanship. It leaves a bad taste in my mouth.

IV

One of the most fascinating recent cases on the establishment clause is *Edwards v. Aguillard*.[18] In this case, the Supreme Court held unconstitu-

14. According to an 1853 report of the Boston School Committee, "The ends of government require that religious instruction be given in our Public Schools." Quoted in Leonard Dinnerstein, Roger L. Nichols, and David M. Reimers, *Natives and Strangers: Blacks, Indians, and Immigrants in America*, 2d ed. (New York: Oxford University Press, 1990).

15. A number of Catholics saw the public schools as "a huge conspiracy against religion, individual liberty and enterprise, and parental rights." Ibid., 175.

16. For a more realistic account of the effect of a Catholic school upbringing, see Garry Wills, "Memories of a Catholic Boyhood," in *Bare Ruined Choirs: Doubt, Prophecy, and Radical Religion* (New York: Delta, 1971).

17. Compare his famous statement in *West Virginia v. Barnette*, 319 U.S. 624 (1943): "If there is any fixed star in our constitutional constellation, it is that no official, high or petty, can prescribe what shall be orthodox in politics, nationalism, religion, or other matters of opinion or force citizens to confess by word or act their faith therein" (642). Those who have not yet read Jackson's *Barnette* opinion should do so; it is splendid.

18. 482 U.S. 578 (1987).

tional a Louisiana statute that bore the title "Balanced Treatment for Creation-Science and Evolution-Science in Public School Instruction." The import of the act is apparent from its title; it would require that the teaching of evolution be balanced with the teaching of creationism. By the Louisiana act, no school is required to teach either evolution or creationism; but if either is taught, both must be taught (*Aguillard*, 580). The status quo ante was that evolution was customarily taught, and so the practical impact of the act was to forbid the teaching of evolution unless it was also accompanied by instruction in "creation science" (586). I wish to consider how this case fits together with *Everson*.

By the time *Aguillard* was decided, forty years had passed since *Everson*, and in those forty years there had been numerous cases in which the court considered the import of the establishment clause. Consequently, one would expect what one finds, that Justice Brennan (writing for the majority) would proceed from rather more recent precedents than *Everson* and that he would not bother to revisit ground that seems uncontested. Even so, I judge that the basic story told in *Everson* is still fundamental to the decision.

The influence of *Everson* is seen most directly in Justice Powell's concurrence. Justice Powell gives a brief history clearly derived from *Everson*; he cites *Everson* explicitly, and his story line reproduces Justice Black's.[19] Omitting the citations, the paragraph reads as follows:

> The history of the Religion Clauses of the First Amendment has been chronicled by this Court in detail. Therefore, only a brief review at this point may be appropriate. The early settlers came to this country from Europe to escape religious persecution that took the form of forced support of state-established churches. The new Americans thus reacted strongly when they perceived the same type of religious intolerance emerging in this country. The reaction in Virginia, the home of many of the Founding Fathers, is instructive. George Mason's draft of the Virginia Declaration of Rights was adopted by the House of Burgesses in 1776. Because of James Madison's influence, the Declaration of Rights embodied the guarantee of *free exercise* of religion, as opposed to *toleration*. Eight years later, a provision prohibiting the establishment of religion became a part of Virginia law when James Madison's Memorial and Remonstrance

---

19. *Aguillard*, 605. He also cites *Engel v. Vitale*, 370 U.S. 421, 425–30 (1962), and *McGowan v. Maryland*, 366 U.S. 420, 437–42 (1961).

against Religious Assessments, written in response to a proposal that all Virginia citizens be taxed to support the teaching of the Christian religion, spurred the legislature to consider and adopt Thomas Jefferson's Bill for Establishing Religious Freedom. Both the guarantees of free exercise and against the establishment of religion were then incorporated into the Federal Bill of Rights by its drafter, James Madison. (*Aguillard*, 605–6)

By the time *Aguillard* is on the docket, the judges who decide establishment-clause cases customarily cite a three-part test, and moreover, many of the cases read as though they actually apply the cited test.[20] The test requires a statute to pass three hurdles. To quote Justice Brennan: "First, the legislature must have adopted the law with a secular purpose. Second, the statute's principal or primary effect must be one that neither advances nor inhibits religion. Third, the statute must not result in an excessive entanglement of government with religion" (*Aguillard*, 583).

The most notable feature of this test is the dichotomy that it establishes between the secular and the religious.[21] There is some irony in the dichotomy between the secular and the religious; after all, it is a commonplace by now to observe that constitutional law is the "civil religion" of the United States.[22] Furthermore, using dichotomies to decide cases is rather passé in modern jurisprudence; academics regularly pronounce that "balancing" is the sine qua non of good judging.[23] Consequently, the use of dichotomies is not inevitable. Perhaps there is some special reason that the judges talk as though there is a sharp distinction between the secular and the religious.

20. The canonical cite for this test is *Lemon v. Kurtzman*, 403 U.S. 602, 612–13 (1971). One may doubt whether the Court actually applied this test in *Lynch v. Donnelly*, 465 U.S. 668 (1984).

21. There are several alternatives. If defining "religion" and "religious" are necessary, one can use the "family resemblance" technique found in Ludwig Wittgenstein's *Philosophical Investigations* (New York: Macmillan, 1968). Alternatively, one can define "an establishment of religion" by way of analogy to particular practices. For an interesting discussion of these possibilities, see George C. Freeman III, "The Misguided Search for the Constitutional Definition of 'Religion,'" 71 *Georgetown L. J.* 1519 (1983).

22. See, e.g., Sanford Levinson, "The Constitution in American Civil Religion," 1979 *Sup. Ct. Rev.* 123. And by the way, Professor Levinson is no heretic; I think that it is no accident that he wrote a book titled *Constitutional Faith*.

23. For a good discussion of this topic, see T. Alexander Aleinikoff, "Constitutional Law in the Age of Balancing," 96 *Yale L. J.* 943 (1987), which is reprinted in part in Aleinikoff's *Modern Constitutional Theory: A Reader*, 2d ed. (St. Paul, Minn.: West Publishing, 1991). By the way, the irony in the text is intentional. I agree that the dichotomies are bad, but "balancing" is not the only alternative; analogical reasoning and "family resemblance" analysis are equally plausible.

I suspect that the principal motive behind accepting this dichotomy is the power of the stories as they were told by Black and Jackson. If religion is as dangerous and disruptive as Black and Jackson have claimed, then of course, to act with a religious purpose instead of a secular purpose is something that is suspect. Furthermore, given the danger, there is a desperate need to maintain the distinction. The consequence of holding this principle—that the dichotomy of secular purposes and religious purposes must be maintained—is that a confrontation between science and religion must be avoided. Curiously enough, it is my memory that when astronomy is taught, the Copernicus story is always told as one of the great confrontations between science and religion. I would think that a conscientious legislator might well see Darwin's challenge as just as fundamental as Copernicus's and conclude that if evolution is taught, the confrontation ought to be squarely faced.[24]

However, I have no criticism of the result. As Justice Brennan quite accurately points out, this statute as drafted does not set up a structure that is fair and evenhanded. Consequently, ignoring purpose for the moment, the effect of the statute is not neutral; the statute seems to fail on the second part of the three-part test. The crucial language on Brennan's opinion is the following:

> Furthermore, the goal of basic "fairness" is hardly furthered by the Act's discriminatory preference for the teaching of creation science and against the teaching of evolution. While requiring that curriculum guides be developed for creation science, the Act says nothing of comparable guides for evolution. . . . Similarly, resource services are supplied for creation science but not for evolution. . . . Only "creation scientists" can serve on the panel that supplies the resource services. . . . The Act forbids school boards to discriminate against anyone who "chooses to be a creation-scientist" or to teach "creationism," but fails to protect those who choose to teach evolution or any other noncreation science theory, or who refuse to teach creation science. (*Aguillard*, 588)

If the decision had rested on these grounds alone, it would be unremarkable, but there is more to the case. First, there is something dubious about

---

24. Once again, my memory of what I was taught, and my observation of what my children have been taught, suggests that this is a routine practice. I am one of those who comes down on Darwin's side on these issues, but I certainly think that if I were teaching the subject I would regard myself as cowardly if I did not confront this conflict.

the court's use of legislative history to identify purpose. Recall that identifying the "purpose" of a statute is the first part of a three-part test. How should purpose be identified? In Justice Brennan's opinion, he cites the words of Senator Keith, the legislative sponsor of the act, and Edward Boudreaux, whom Brennan characterizes as the chief witness at committee hearings (591–92). To be sure, this evidence is relevant; but what seems wrong is that Brennan appears to make it decisive. Justice Brennan makes no attempt to ask if those who voted in favor of the act did so for the same reasons, or for different reasons.

Brennan's technique of using only the sponsor's views, to the exclusion of the rest of the legislature, is logically dubious. If the Louisiana legislature is like any other group of humans, we can infer diversity. In the absence of evidence to the contrary, I would assume substantial diversity, and yet Brennan does not address the possibility. He seems to be following Justice Black's technique in the *Everson* case. For Black, only Madison's views had legal status; for Brennan, the same is true for Senator Keith. With both Black and Brennan, there is disquieting contempt toward all other participants in the process. I hasten to add, however, that I believe that Brennan's ultimate conclusion is correct. As I have already noted, the act discriminated against those who would teach "evolution-science" in favor of those who would teach "creation-science." Perhaps others would differ, but I would argue that the best evidence for one's purpose is the fact of what one does. Consequently, I do not wish to criticize Brennan's conclusion about the purpose of the act. I bring up the use of legislative history for a different reason, which is, the disquieting similarity between what Brennan has done in this case and what Black did in the *Everson* case.

The second disquieting feature of the majority opinion is the dictum concerning the future. The dictum occurs in the way that it generally does in these sorts of opinions; once the judges have said that the legislature cannot do what they did, they customarily go on to say that of course there are many other reasonable things the legislature could have done. The relevant parts of Brennan's opinion in which he enacts the "open door scenario" for the future reads as follows: "We do not imply that a legislature could never require that scientific critiques of prevailing scientific theories be taught. . . . [T]eaching a variety of scientific theories about the origins of humankind to schoolchildren might be validly done with the clear secular intent of enhancing the effectiveness of science instruction" (593–94).

The obvious query is, Why should only scientific critiques of scientific theories be taught? Recall that the teaching of astronomy and cosmology

always entails the teaching of the historical confrontation between Copernicus and Galileo and the Papacy. Should we sweep under the rug the massive
controversy unleashed by Darwin's famous book? Unless the public schools
are to be devoted solely to indoctrination,[25] controversies should be taught
as controversies. The scientists I know criticize creationism as being nonsci-
entific because it is nontestable. It seems to me that this is a very fine thing
to be teaching, but what sort of response would the creationist make? More
generally, what sort of response would one make who rejects this particular
scientific critique of religion?[26] However, these criticisms of *Aguillard* must
not be overemphasized. The point of criticizing is *not* to suggest that there
are errors of logic or reasoning; the point is to become more self-conscious
of the possibility that the logic and reasoning of the opinion are driven by
a story that supports the logic, that makes the logic seem logical. I suggest
that *Aguillard* rests on the story of *Everson* and that one is more likely to be
persuaded by the reasoning of *Aguillard* if one is also persuaded by *Everson*.

V

Finally, one must face up to the question, What is good and bad about
these stories? As I see it, answering this question demands that we imagine
the alternatives. In ethical matters, "ought implies can"; it makes no sense
to criticize what is done unless there is a better alternative. We can imagine
alternatives in two ways. First, one can contrast storytelling with something
else and ask, Are there alternatives to telling stories? Are these alternatives
better or worse than storytelling? In short, one could endorse storytelling
either because there is no practical alternative or because storytelling is the
best alternative. Second, what alternative stories can be told? Given that

---

25. See pages 28–31 above.
26. See Stanley L. Jaki, *The Origin of Science and the Science of Its Origin* (South Bend, Ind.:
Regnery/Gateway, 1979), in which the author concludes that science takes on its proper perspective
only when the origin of all is placed in the creative act of God. For an argument that there are no
logically compelling grounds to accept the predictive power and practical applicability of scientific
knowledge as truth, and that to accept truth by reference to the criteria of efficacy requires an act
of faith, see Leszek Kolakowski, *Religion, If There Is No God: On God, the Devil, Sin and Other
Worries of the So-Called Philosophy of Religion* (New York: Oxford University Press, 1983). I do not
agree with the theses of these two books, but I do not understand why it would be unconstitutional to
teach them in a biology class.

judges tell stories to persuade, do we wish to accept or reject the particular stories that they advance?

I address these questions in Chapter 5 of this book. In this chapter, I wish to suggest a few preliminary conclusions that may prepare the way. For example, what conclusions might be plausible about the issue of alternative stories? In particular, what alternative story might one tell about the relationship between Darwinism and the establishment clause? I am not a communicant, and so I shall not tell the better stories from the religious point of view. Indeed, I am a devout Darwinian,[27] and so my question would be, How does one tell this story from the Darwinian point of view?

Note first that a Darwinian account of phenomena must be a narrative.[28] In a Darwinian account, random accident can change the course of the future. Mutations are produced randomly, and if the mutant and its progeny are better at gathering food, then the character of the species will be altered. Furthermore, the evolutionary change of a species is a one-way street. If a change is a short-term success, but a long-range disaster, there is no way to back up and correct the change. Indeed, most of these one-way streets have dead-ended with extinction.[29]

The next distinction that can be offered is that between Darwinian accounts of evolution and non-Darwinian accounts. I emphasize this distinction because it is not as sharp in the popular mind as it is among biologists. It is well known in the trade, although less well known in the culture at large, that the Darwinian revolution in evolution did not occur until the middle years of our own century; in the nineteenth century, Darwin's own, evolutionary ideas triumphed, but they were generally non-Darwinian in content.[30] The non-Darwinian accounts were built on the key concepts of "trends" and "progress." It seemed obvious and beyond question to Darwin's contemporaries that men were higher and beasts were lower and that the inevitable trend of progress must have been from lower to higher. His contemporaries might have been able to abandon the concept of divine guidance; they were not able to abandon the concept of destiny. Darwin himself

---

27. I use the word "devout" advisedly. Ecclesiastes has been for most of my life the book of the Bible which speaks most powerfully to me. My Darwinism fits well with the theology of this book.

28. See Peter J. Bowler, "Narrative Structure of Theories," in *Theories of Human Evolution: A Century of Debate, 1844–1944* (Baltimore: Johns Hopkins University Press, 1986), 314. See also Gillian Beer, *Darwin's Plots: Evolutionary Narrative in Darwin, George Eliot, and Nineteenth-Century Fiction* (London: Routledge & Kegan Paul, 1983).

29. Stephen Jay Gould, *Ever Since Darwin: Reflections in Natural History* (New York: Norton, 1977).

30. See Bowler, *Theories of Human Evolution.*

was more cautious. In his famous book, *The Origin of Species*, the word "evolution" appears only in the last paragraph. It seems that Darwin wished to distance himself from the conceptualization of "evolution" as "progress."

Let me give an example. A large number of scholars have argued that a crucial step in the evolutionary changes of primates occurred when our ancestors moved out of the forest and onto the plains. An example of a non-Darwinian account of this move is the following:

> In one group the distinctively Primate process of growth and special-ization of the brain, which had been going on in their ancestors for many thousands, even millions, of years, reached the stage where the more venturesome members of the group—stimulated perhaps by some local failure of the customary food, or maybe led forth by curiosity bred of their growing realization of the possibilities of the unknown world beyond the trees, which had hither to been their home—were impelled to issue forth from their forests, and seek new sources of food and new surroundings on hill and plain. The other group, perhaps because they happened to be more favorably situated or attuned to their surroundings, living in a land of plenty, which encouraged indolence and habit and stagnation of efforts in growth, were free from this glorious unrest, and remained apes.[31]

In this passage, we see that the growth of the brain is being postulated as an inevitable trend. Our primate ancestors had remained in the forest, and while they were there, the brain became ever larger, ever more specialized, ever more intelligent. Finally, this intelligent creature saw a new opportu-nity and through its splendid initiative escaped from the forest. The alterna-tive Darwinian account would be that our primate ancestors were forced out of the forest (presumably by environmental and climatic changes?) and that life on the plains then led (perhaps from tool making? or a greater threat from predators? or the scarcity of food?) to a change in brain size. In short, the issue is whether a change in intelligence led a primate to seek a change in environment; or whether a change in environment led to a change in the primate's intelligence. The Darwinian account clearly supports a choice for the latter thesis.[32] This particular example can be generalized in

---

31. G. E. Smith, *The Evolution of Man* (1924), as quoted in ibid., 169–70.

32. Needless to say, I do not intend to assert which Darwinian account is the best one, and I certainly don't know whether the forest-grasslands transition is key. For an argument that the crucial

various ways, but I have obviously chosen it for polemical reasons. The passage previously quoted, of our primate ancestors escaping from the forests into the grassland of the plains, is a story that reads exactly like Justice Black's story in *Everson*. In Black's story, there is also an escape, and in Black's story, the escape is also a consequence of intelligence and initiative. Both stories are lovely; both are non-Darwinian.

An alternative account would emphasize contingency, not destiny. For example, let me take just one detail of Black's story, that is, Madison's success in the Virginia legislature. I would begin by noting that Madison was not the first to argue the thesis he advanced; he put together his argument by recombining the extant material of his culture. Having made a novel arrangement of older material, Madison then offered it to his contemporaries, and it was accepted. Presumably, there are differences in the environment; these differences were the product of other changes that may or may not have had anything to do with religion; and because Madison's argument was made in a new environment, it succeeded where its predecessors had failed. At this point in the story, one needs to identify the contingent facts, the changes in the environment that made it possible for an argument to succeed and for something new to come into the world. What was this something new? My own suspicion is that it was a tax revolt, but I do not wish to push this thesis. I am not as interested in telling this particular story as I am in illustrating the form that good stories ought to take.[33]

One of the most intriguing ironies of the *Aguillard* case is Justice Powell's dictum for the future, that is, his "open door scenario," in which he tells the legislature about the many things they can do:

> As a matter of history, schoolchildren can and should properly be informed of all aspects of this Nation's religious heritage. I would see no constitutional problem if schoolchildren were taught the nature of the Founding Fathers' religious beliefs and how these beliefs affected the attitudes of the times and the structure of our government (*Aguillard*, 606–7).

---

evolution was the consequence of living next to streams and swamps, see Christopher Knight, *Blood Relations* (New Haven: Yale University Press, 1991).

33. A vast question, which is beyond the scope of this essay, is, What are the narrative tropes for Darwinian fictions? In *Darwin's Plots* Gillian Beer proposes that Eliot's use of Darwin initiates a new epoch in the history of the novel. Unfortunately, I am incompetent to judge.

I see "no constitutional problem" in teaching such things either, but there are two gentle ironies to be noted. The first is a contrast between Powell's dictum and his opinion, which I quoted earlier. In the opinion, Powell aligned himself with Justice Black's story, in which the Deistic ideals of the Enlightenment are critical to our founding. But in the passage just cited, he allows that religious ideas may be crucial to our founding. If this be so, and it is, then the simplistic tale that was told in *Everson* must be modified. The second irony is that this elegiac passage occurs in an opinion in which the Darwinian triumph is being constitutionalized. Justice Powell writes as though he is not aware (and perhaps he is not) that part of the attack on Darwinism in the nineteenth century came from those who feared that the impact of Darwinism on "the structure of our government" would be debilitating.[34] Furthermore, he seems unaware of the impact of Darwinian thought on the stories that are told about law.

Most of the "mainstream" stories about law are evolutionary but non-Darwinian. Take Holmes for example. We have all heard the famous aphorism from his *Common Law*, "The life of the law has not been logic: it has been experience."[35] To study experience, we study history, and so Holmes says, "In order to know what it [the law] is, we must know what it has been, and what it tends to become."[36] I hope that the reader trembled at reading the clause, "what it tends to become." "Trends" are not random, and they prevail for reasons that are not contingent; and if there are inevitable trends, then accidental features of the fit between act and environment cannot rechannel destiny. For Holmes, there is destiny; for a Darwinian, there is chance. Holmes ends his first chapter of *The Common Law* with the following:

While the terminology of morals is still retained [in the law], and while the law does still and always, in a certain sense, measure legal liability by moral standards, it nevertheless, by the very necessity of its nature, is continually transmuting those moral standards into external or objective ones, from which the actual guilt of the party concerned is wholly eliminated.[37]

34. See Bowler, *Theories of Human Evolution*, 41–58.
35. Oliver Wendell Holmes Jr., *The Common Law* (Boston: Little, Brown, 1923), 1.
36. Ibid.
37. Ibid., 33.

The truth or falsity of Holmes's story is not the point. We could, indeed,
tell the story the other way around—we could say that the growth of civiliza-
tion has led us away from objective standards toward subjective ones. But
tell it either way, one is still telling the story of "onward and upward." Either
way, it is a non-Darwinian story.

I end on this Holmesian note because I believe that lawyers and judges
are addicted to this type of story. When lawyers and judges tell stories about
legal change, they do not say "change," they say "growth" or "development."
When they tell the story of "growth" (recall Holmes's metaphor—"the *life*
of the law*"), it always turns out to be a story about onward and upward.
Consequently, I fear the recent scholarly fashion of praising narrative and
asserting that narrative is morally superior to theory.[38] I too would like more
narrative and less theory, but if lawyers and judges read this recent fashion
as ratifying the sort of story they would customarily tell, then the consequences will be bad.

However, these particular criticisms of the stories told in *Everson* and
Aguillard are rather narrow and do not address the larger question: Can we
eliminate these fictions? Can our stories be solidly factual? I think not. At
law, we are not allowed the luxury of refusing to come to a decision because
we do not have enough facts. We have to fill in the gaps, and in doing so,
I suspect that we will almost always tell fictional stories.

38. See the symposium at the University of Michigan on legal storytelling, 87 *Mich. L. Rev.*
2073–2494 (1989). Nancy L. Cook has an article, "Outside the Tradition: Literature as Legal
Scholarship," forthcoming in the *University of Cincinnati Law Review*, that is a thorough and
sympathetic review of the current academic praise of storytelling.

2

The Story of Limits

Marbury v. Madison[1] is one of those cases that most people have heard about; indeed, many lawyers think it is the very foundation of our legal system. *Marbury's* significance rests on its contribution to the judiciary's power. In many nations, the national judiciary is one of the weaker branches of government; in the United States, the national judiciary is strong and self-confident. This strength and self-confidence was not generated in a single day by a single case; *Marbury* alone did not create the Supreme Court that we know today. However, this case has become a symbol; when historians present their analyses and describe how the judiciary has become so important, *Marbury* has the place of honor.

If our judges are far more powerful than the judges of other nations, and

---

1. 1 Cranch 137 (1803).

if *Marbury v. Madison* was one of those extraordinary events that led the way toward this unique state of affairs, then the opinion in this case should capture our attention. Let us, therefore, examine the fictions that have made Marshall persuasive, and in order to see why these fictions were so potent, let us begin with the historical context.

I

When the story begins,[2] John Marshall was not on the Supreme Court. He was, however, one of the leading members of the Federalist party and was serving as secretary of state. Although Marshall held a responsible position in his party, his party's prospects did not seem good. The Federalists had just suffered an overwhelming defeat in the last election; Thomas Jefferson's Republican party had captured a majority in both houses of Congress as well as the presidency. Consequently, as the story begins, Marshall is serving out the last months of a "lame duck" administration. The lame duck Federalists were not inactive. Having lost their grip on the legislative and executive branches of the national government, they were trying to preserve their power over the judicial branch. They passed legislation that expanded the size of the judiciary by creating new courts and new judgeships and then proceeded to fill these posts with members of their own party. During this flurry of activity, President Adams also had to consider a Supreme Court appointment. Oliver Ellsworth, who had served as the third chief justice, had stepped down in September 1800, shortly before the elections. Adams's first choice for the office was John Jay, who had served as the first chief justice, but Jay refused.

Jay refused the nomination because he feared that the job offered too little in the way of useful power.[3] Jay stated that the institutional structure of the Supreme Court (and indeed, of the entire judiciary) was defective, and in fact Jay's assertion was reasonable. The jurisdiction of the court was limited, and one could say that the first decade had not been promising. The Supreme Court had decided only one major constitutional case, *Chisholm v.*

2. There are many accounts of this case, but the most important are William Winslow Crosskey, *Politics and the Constitution in the History of the United States* (Chicago: University of Chicago Press, 1953), and Dumas Malone, *Jefferson and His Time*, 6 vols. (Boston: Little, Brown, 1948–74).

3. See Jay's letter to John Adams in *The Correspondence and Public Papers of John Jay*, ed. Henry P. Johnston (New York: G. P. Putnam's Sons, 1893), 4:285.

Georgia,[4] and it had been promptly overruled by the Eleventh Amendment. One can understand why Jay might be skeptical. Although Jay refused, Marshall did not. He accepted the offer and was duly nominated, confirmed, and appointed. Since the time left to his administration was short, President Adams did not want to select a new secretary of state, and so Marshall held both jobs until the calendar ran out. In the twilight of Adams's term, the events that precipitated the *Marbury* case were set in motion.

The lawsuit was precipitated by an act of Congress that provided for magistrates for the District of Columbia. This statute did not designate the number of magistrates that were to be appointed; instead, the president was given discretion to say how many were needed. Adams decided that the district could use forty-two magistrates, so he generated a list and sent it to the Senate, where the requisite advice and consent was given. Unfortunately, it is not altogether clear what happened next. We do not know exactly what steps were taken to complete the appointment process. The most common interpretation of the facts is that the necessary documents were prepared, submitted to President Adams, signed, and sent to Secretary of State Marshall's office, where they lay. Given the press of business, they may or may not have been sealed with the great seal of the United States. At any rate, and regardless of whether the commissions were sealed, they were never delivered. The clerks and runners of the department did not give Marbury his commission; Marbury sued the new secretary of state, James Madison, asking that his commission be delivered.

Perhaps I should pause at this point and reflect on the story I have just told. I have purported to give an account of the "historical context" in which this case arose. Is my story a fiction? Or is it based on the facts? In part, I cannot say because I am not competent to judge. I have taken my account from the standard histories; I have not examined the sources. However, in part I can judge, since I do know something about how history is done, and I know something about the fuzziness of the line between fact and fiction. My own opinion is that we need to remember that the words "fact" and "fiction" are ordinary words that are used daily in routine and ordinary conversations. Consequently, they have as many different meanings as they have different uses. We cannot draw sharp boundaries to restrict their meanings; we cannot assume that these words mark off a sharp dichotomy. Furthermore, I doubt whether we can stipulate precision, since there is no theoretical justification for precision. We could theorize a precise distinction

---

4. 2 Dallas 419 (1793). Jay was chief justice and a member of the majority in that case.

between fact and fiction in history if we had a good theory about the proper way to do history. Unfortunately, we don't. To be sure, I am only an amateur, and so my belief that we lack a comprehensive theory of history may be a function of my ignorance. But it does seem to be true that history differs from mathematics. Mathematicians agree that certain mathematical fundamentals—for example, that there are an infinite number of prime numbers—have been proved. Historians must live with the knowledge that certain historical fundamentals—such as the cause(s) of the Civil War— can never be proved.

Given that we don't have a precise definition of fact versus fiction, we fall back to rough and ready tests. What sort of evidence do we have? Is there reason to doubt it? Is there reason to believe it? What types of inferences do we have to make? How reliable are these inferences? And so forth. Depending on how we answer these questions, we draw the line. Depending on how we answer these questions, we conclude that certain sentences in a story are either "based on facts" or else "produced by the imagination." Using these tests, one can note that most of the story rests on creditable public documents. We can accept as facts the defeat of Adams and the election of Jefferson, and similarly, the statements that Congress passed certain statutes, that Adams submitted certain names to the Senate, and so forth, can all be justly called facts. I suppose that there are various reasons to say that these are actually statements of facts, but I call them facts because I can't think of any reason to doubt them. Furthermore, we can trust the standard story about the political response to this attempt to make Mr. Marbury a magistrate. The Jeffersonian Republicans were outraged. We know that they were outraged because they said they were, they acted as if they were, and it is sensible that they would have been. Jefferson himself ordered his new secretary of state, James Madison, not to deliver the undelivered commissions. Jefferson then determined that the District of Columbia needed only thirty magistrates, instead of the forty-two that Adams had designated, and so he restarted the process with a list of thirty, twenty-five of whom were drawn from Adams's list. Marbury was not included, and so he sued.

When Marbury sued, his first problem was figuring out where to sue. In modern times, a disappointed office seeker who wishes to sue would know which court to use, but Marbury had a problem, which arises out of the history of the judiciary. The statute establishing the national judiciary was only eleven years old. In the first Congress, in the first session, a committee was appointed in the Senate to draft a judiciary act; this committee was appointed on the day after a quorum had been achieved.[5] At the time of drafting, the Congress was then sitting in New York and the District of Columbia had not yet been envisioned. Consequently, national courts were established in the several states but none were established for the nonexistent and unimagined District of Columbia.

The decision to move the national capital to the banks of the Potomac was not made until two years later during the summer of 1791. Although it may seem to be a digression, let me explain the move, since it is part of the context of Marbury's case. The decision to move was made at the second session of the first Congress, and it was one of the political deals and compromises of that session. The political divisions behind the disputes of 1791 were still alive when Marbury filed his lawsuit, and furthermore, these divisions shaped much of what happened.

In 1791, the members of Congress addressed the fiscal problems of the nation. The agenda was set by Alexander Hamilton, the secretary of the treasury, who issued three reports in which he proposed schemes for funding the public debt, for establishing a national bank, and for creating tariffs to encourage manufacturing. These three reports were as controversial as they were brilliant, and they generated the first major political division in the new government. One possible interpretation of the events is that the political division generated by Hamilton's proposal led in time to the creation of the two political parties, the Federalists and the Republicans. Hamilton won on two of the three issues (funding the debt and establishing the bank), but ten years later, the Jeffersonian Republicans prevailed, the Federalist party was defeated, and the events that triggered Marbury's case were generated.

The first order of business was the scheme for funding the public debt. Although Hamilton won, a political deal was necessary. James Madison, then a member of the House of Representatives and later to be the defendant in Marbury's case, led the opposition. Madison charged that northern speculators would be the primary and perhaps the only beneficiaries of Hamilton's funding scheme. These charges were politically powerful; Madison was also skilled at parliamentary maneuvers and deadlocked Congress on the issue. In desperation, Alexander Hamilton turned to Thomas Jefferson, who was then the secretary of state and who would later as president order Madison not to deliver Marbury's commission. Hamilton thought that the union

---

5. Wilfred J. Ritz, *Rewriting the History of the Judiciary Act of 1789: Exposing Myths, Challenging Premises, and Using New Evidence*, ed. L. H. LaRue and Wythe Holt (Norman: University of Oklahoma Press, 1989), 13.

itself was endangered by this deadlock, and he asked Jefferson for help. Two days later, Hamilton, Jefferson, and Madison sat down together and cut a deal. Madison ceased to oppose Hamilton's scheme for the funding of the public debt and Hamilton agreed to move the capital to the banks of the Potomac. For an interim period of ten years, while land was acquired and buildings constructed, the national capital was to be moved from New York and located in Philadelphia. The funding bill was passed. However, a detail was overlooked. What about the judiciary? Would it be a good idea to amend the Judiciary Act, which had passed two years earlier, to provide for the new District of Columbia? The question does not appear to have been asked, and therefore, it was not answered.

Construction began on the White House and the Capitol in 1792, but progress was slow. The parade to Washington began in June 1800. Adams and his family moved into the White House (it was not then called by that name) on November 1, 1800, although neither the Capitol nor the White House was finished. Within a few days, the election was held, and Adams lost. As described above, the lame duck Federalists turned their attention to the judiciary.[6]

With the above as background, we can see that the historical context of Marbury's case includes more than just the election of 1800; it also includes the political deal of 1791 to move the capital to the Potomac. The election of 1800 made the Federalists a lame duck party, and it thus set off the maneuvering that led to the case. However, the political divisions that were powerful in 1800 were partially generated by the political disputes of 1791. Furthermore, had the Congress in 1791 anticipated the problem for the judiciary in moving to the Potomac, the shape of events would have been different. If Congress had amended the Judiciary Act to provide for judges for the newly established District of Columbia, then perhaps the Federalist would not have passed an act in 1800 that provided for a new set of magistrates for the District. Alternatively, perhaps they would have, but at least there would have been courts established in the District to which Marbury could have brought this suit. As it was, he sued in the only place that seemed plausible, the United States Supreme Court.

(As an aside, let me note that I have constructed the story to emphasize its contingency. Marbury was forced to bring his lawsuit in the Supreme Court because the rather untidy compromises that resulted in the Judiciary

6. See David Burner, Eugene D. Genovese, and Forrest McDonald, *The American People* (New York: Revisionary Press, 1980), 116–20, 128–30, 139–41.

Act of 1789 did not establish any courts for the District of Columbia, and this oversight was reasonable enough because in 1789 there were as of yet no plans for moving the government from New York. The decision to move was not made until 1791, and was part of a rather untidy compromise over funding the national debt. By the standards of political compromises, the Judiciary Act and the decision to move the capital were fairly coherent; however, they did not fit together too well, and indeed, it would have been a miracle if they had. We should not expect a series of human actions to fit together logically unless the actors are following some plan, and we should not expect to find a plan in a series of political compromises.)

II

Let me now turn to the case itself. It would be possible to give more details about the events that were precipitated by Marbury's lawsuit.[7] However, I would like to shift now to John Marshall's opinion in the case. Marshall describes the history of the case, and like most judicial stories about the history of a case, Marshall's story uses technical language. Since Marshall uses only two sentences to tell the story, decoding this technical language will not be a lengthy process.

> At the last term on the affidavits then read and filed with the clerk, a rule was granted in this case, requiring the secretary of state to show cause why a mandamus should not issue, directing him to deliver to William Marbury his commission as a justice of the peace for the county of Washington, in the district of Columbia.
>
> No cause has been shown, and the present motion is for a mandamus. (*Marbury*, 153–54)

Let us now decode, starting with the phrase "at the last term." In the early days of the republic, courts were not open for business throughout the year; instead, the legislation that established the courts set forth the "terms of court," which were allotted portions of the calendar during which the court could do business. By way of comparison, one might consider the average state legislature, which can only do business during its allotted

---

7. Dumas Malone's account in *Jefferson and His Time* has not yet been surpassed.

sessions. Just as today, legislators cannot assemble and pass laws unless they are "in session," so then judges could not decide cases unless they were sitting during a "term of court." Consequently, when Marshall uses the phrase, "at the last term," he is speaking within a tradition that has become somewhat remote to us. However, his bland words also conceal some rather startling historical events. The "last term" was the December term of 1801, yet Marshall is writing during the February term of 1803. There is a gap, and it was created by the Congress. As I have just pointed out, the Congress had authority to establish terms of court; and what Congress can establish, it can abolish; and it had done so. When Marbury filed his suit, and when the judges began to act on it, the Congress abolished the next several terms of court to prevent immediate action on this lawsuit. But Marshall's bland description conceals these events by ignoring them.

After the phrase, "At the last term," Marshall's first sentence has the phrase "on the affidavits then read and filed with the clerk. . . ." An "affidavit" is a document which is sworn to under oath, and the phrase quoted informs us that this type of document was filed with the clerk of the court and read by the judges. (Or perhaps affidavits were read aloud in court by counsel.) However, Marshall's opening sentence does not state what sort of document these affidavits claim to support. In current practice, one starts a lawsuit by filing a "complaint," and in some cases (not all) one might file affidavits in support of the allegations of the complaint. Was there a document analogous to our modern "complaint"? There was, but we must turn back to the court reporter's statements to find out what it was, and if we do turn back, we discover that the case was started by filing a "motion" (137–38).

I think that this detail, that the case started with a "motion," is an important clue, in that it shows that Marbury's lawyer not only was in quandary about which court would be the proper forum for his lawsuit, but also had problems with selecting the proper procedure. Furthermore, these technical uncertainties are emblematic of the larger uncertainties of power, of the allocations of power among the legislature, and executive, and the judiciary. We can see how these technical uncertainties link up with the larger uncertainties about power if we turn to the court reporter's description of the procedural maneuvering. The reporter, William Cranch, describes how the case began, and the details of his description are fascinating. It is even more fascinating to speculate on why Marshall did not discuss these details during the course of his opinion. According to Cranch, there were four plaintiffs in the case: William Marbury, Dennis Ramsay, Robert Townsend Hooe [sic], and William Harper. Their attorney was Charles Lee, and Cranch describes the case by starting with Lee's summary of the affidavits. All of this is routine enough, and the description of the contents of the affidavits is similarly routine. (It is also rather boring.) The contents are described abstractly, and they state no more than the legal conclusions of nomination, advice and consent, preparation of commission, and so forth. The more detailed facts of who did what, when, where, and how are not specified.

However, it gets interesting rather quickly, for Cranch represents Lee as stating that he has been "much embarrassed" in his attempt to obtain evidence in support of the affidavits. Lee states that he had asked the Senate by way of "a respectful memorial" to permit their secretary to make extracts from the journals so that he could show that Marbury and the other plaintiffs had indeed been nominated by the president and that the Senate had indeed advised and consented to their appointment. The Senate had refused. Furthermore, Lee states that he had attempted to obtain affidavits from clerks of the secretary of state's office, which evidence is presumably being sought to show that a commission was in fact prepared, signed, and sealed. But they refused to give him their affidavits. In short, the executive and the legislature were refusing to cooperate in the production of evidence, from which one might infer that they had no intention of cooperating in more significant ways (138–39).

We arrive thus at the first critical impasse in the case. According to Cranch, Lee then called as witnesses Jacob Wagner and Daniel Brent. (We are told that they had been summoned to appear, but we are not told by Cranch what procedure was used to issue the summons.) However, these two witnesses objected to being sworn, and Cranch states that they did so on the grounds that "they were clerks in the Department of State and not bound to disclose any facts relating to the business or transactions in the office" (139). What should be done? Not only have the clerks refused to cooperate out of court, but now that they are summoned to court, they assert that they have no obligation to testify. However, Lee was surely not surprised by their lack of cooperation, and he presented an argument in support of his positions that the clerks must testify (139–42). The bulk of Lee's argument was devoted to describing the statutory provisions creating and regulating the Department of State, but the core of his argument is his distinction between those duties imposed on the secretary by law and those duties imposed on the secretary by the will of the president. Lee conceded that "facts concerning foreign correspondencies, and confidential communications between the head of the Department and the President" could not be inquired into (142). However, Lee argued that the secretary was bound to produce such documents as grants of title from the United States to an individual or a private act on behalf of the individual, and Lee further argued that if the documents were bound to be recorded and produced, then one could examine the clerks in a court of law to determine if such documents in fact existed.

The court ruled in Lee's favor, and the witnesses were ordered to be sworn. Unfortunately, this moment of high drama tapers off inconclusively. We are told that the questions were presented to the witnesses in writing, from which one can surmise that they were not subjected to sharp and detailed questioning. I make this surmise because the answers, as summarized by Cranch, seem vague; the details of who did what, and when, are never spelled out. One can infer from the testimony that it is more probable than not that the requisite commissions were signed and sealed, but this is merely an inference, since no one states it directly (142–46). After Cranch describes several days of inconclusive maneuvering concerning the witnesses, his account trails off into a rather dry summary of Lee's argument (146–53). In retrospect, the most interesting feature of Lee's argument is that Lee was the only counsel who argued. It appears that the attorney general of the United States did not show up. To be sure, one could say that the only issue before the court was whether papers should be served on the secretary of state, and in this context, it may well be that the attorney general had nothing particular to offer. However, one can read Lee's argument as traversing broadly across the merits of the case; and furthermore, one would think that even the procedural questions raise broad issues on which the attorney general should be heard. With these comments in mind, let us return to John Marshall's opening sentence in his opinion.

As we take up Marshall's opinion once more, perhaps it is worthwhile to translate the eighteenth-century terminology into a more modern jargon. We know that a "motion" supported by "affidavits" was made that a "rule to show cause" should be issued by the court and that the "cause" that is to be shown is "why a mandamus should not issue." Marshall stated that "no cause has been shown" and that a second motion has now been made to the court, which is, that a mandamus should be directed to the secretary of state to deliver the commission (154). How do we translate all of this into modern terms? Recall that the case starts with a "motion." Since this piece of paper, together with its supporting affidavits, was the document filed to begin the lawsuit, let us say that it resembles what we moderns call "the complaint." We generally call the document that initiates a lawsuit the complaint. What then is this strange creature, a "rule to show cause"? In context, it seems plain that the word "rule" is synonymous with the word "order." In other words, the secretary of state is ordered to "show cause." And I think it is tolerably clear that "to show cause" is to do nothing more than what we moderns would call "to answer." If I can summarize all of this as briefly as possible, it appears that Marbury filed a complaint, and that the Supreme Court ordered Madison to file an answer.

I have made such a detailed inquiry into the ancient forms of procedure because I think the decorous language conceals one of the crucial facts about the case. Recall that the second sentence of Marshall's opinion begins "No cause has been shown. . . ." The reader is now in a position to translate these innocuous yet portentous words. If "to show cause" is "to answer," then Marshall has just informed us that the secretary of state and the attorney general have not filed an answer to the complaint. In short, they are ignoring the lawsuit.

Recall my discussion of the facts of this case as they are revealed in William Cranch's summary. Charles Lee was unable to get documents from the Senate or the secretary that would prove his allegations. He summoned clerks from the secretary's office who objected to being sworn. The witnesses were sworn, but they gave vague answers. And throughout these preliminary proceedings, there was no official appearance by the attorney general on behalf of the secretary of state. This pattern of recalcitrance is now, we are told in Marshall's opinion, extended one step further; even after the secretary of state is ordered to file an answer, he refuses to do so. So what is Marshall to do?

The most important thing that Marshall did was to write as though there was no need to describe the political controversy behind the case. I have spent most of this chapter trying to build a sense of drama, to show a confrontation, to write my own fiction of this case. But Marshall tried to remove the drama by giving a dry, procedural description of the events. I have stated that the secretary of state refused to obey John Marshall's order to answer the complaint, and furthermore, that the attorney general did not even bother to show up in court and defend. John Marshall states: "No cause has been shown . . ." (154).

Marshall's dry legalism is the key to his authority, since he can only win this confrontation by fighting on favorable terrain and by exercising great skill in judging what he can safely do. Had he been reckless, it would not have mattered what he said. Rhetoric can do only so much. Even so, his language has the power to persuade, and I hope to show how legalisms can be persuasive, if this legal vocabulary is joined to skillful action, and one must acknowledge that Marshall acted skillfully.

Recall that Marshall was made chief justice by a lame duck president and Senate. To be blunt, the process was rather shabby. William Marbury would have also been a lame duck appointment, but the Federalists weren't efficient enough. Political feelings were intense, and consequently, Marshall could be sure that anything he did would be subject to intense political scrutiny. Furthermore, Marshall knew that James Madison, the secretary of state, had refused to file an answer, and that Levi Lincoln, the attorney general, had not bothered to appear and argue the case. What should Marshall have inferred from the facts? Unless he were an utter fool (and he was not), he would surely infer that Thomas Jefferson, the president, approved of what Madison and Lincoln had done (or, if you prefer, had *not* done). And if Jefferson approved of their defying the Court so far, was it likely that Jefferson and Madison would respond to a court order to deliver Marbury's commission? Surely not.[8]

Since Marshall was politically astute enough to know that Jefferson and Madison would not obey his orders, he also surely understood politics well enough to know that he would be the loser in any political battle that followed. He could expect the Congress to support the president. Congress had made this clear by abolishing a term of court (which prevented any further judicial action) once Marshall's court had issued the order "to show cause." Furthermore, he could expect the people to support the president and the Congress, given the recent electoral repudiation of the Federalist party. And one must remember that Marshall had no accumulated prestige of office to draw upon. He himself was a new judge and his title to the post was tarnished by the shabby political maneuver that had given him the job. The Court was just barely more than a decade old, and in that brief period it had run through three chief justices; recall that John Jay would not accept reappointment because of the all too apparent weaknesses of the court. It is reasonable to suppose that most people shared John Jay's low opinion of the Supreme Court, and further, that John Marshall understood this. In short, Marshall had few assets and many liabilities.

Even so, to back down would be most distasteful. To do so would be to confirm that Marbury (and by implication, himself) had no just claim to his office. Both Marshall and Marbury had been appointed by a lame duck

8. Both Dumas Malone and Merrill Peterson have written that Jefferson would have ignored any such order, and they also believe that the public would have supported Jefferson, not Marshall.

president and confirmed by a lame duck Senate; if Marbury's claim was tarnished, then so was Marshall's. And there were even more important issues at stake, issues far more important that the individual probity of Marbury and Marshall. One of these was the future of the judiciary in the young republic. If Marshall backed down, he had every reason to fear that the judiciary would suffer, that John Jay's skepticism would be ratified.

This was Marshall's dilemma: if he issued an order to deliver the commission, he and the Court would take a beating; if he backed down, he and the Court would take a beating. For someone such as you or I, there would be no way out, but John Marshall was not cut to our small cloth. He reread the statute that was supposedly the basis of the Supreme Court's jurisdiction over the case and decided that it was unconstitutional. He informed Congress that it could not force the Supreme Court to take this case and dismissed it! Of course, the members of Congress did not want him to take the case, and so there was nothing practical they could do to reverse his ruling. Marshall had asserted the power to do nothing, and since nothing was what they wanted him to do, they were powerless to reverse him.

I have just told a fine story about how clever Marshall was, and I freely admit that there are some bad fictions in it. The biggest defect in my story is that I have made Marshall too calculating, too self-conscious about his maneuvers, too Machiavellian. Surely that is not right; it is far more likely that Marshall's mind worked in ways more complicated, and less conscious, than my simplistic account suggests. However, I did not make up this fine story. I have only retold it, in its simplest form, to set the stage for my own analysis.[9]

Let us accept that the brilliance of Marshall's opinion is that he declared a broad power in order to avoid exercising power, and got away with it because "not acting" was the action everyone desired. "Winning by losing" makes a fine story, but why then is Marshall's opinion so persuasive? I suggest that we try to imagine an opinion that would not have been so persuasive. As an aid to one's imagination, I suggest the following exercise: how could one change Marshall's opinion as little as possible and yet totally destroy its persuasive power? I suggest merely changing the opening passages would do it. Suppose Marshall had begun by describing some of the facts I

9. See Fred Rodell, *Nine Men* (New York: Random House, 1955), 86–90. For a more sophisticated, yet analogous, account, see Robert G. McCloskey, *The American Supreme Court* (Chicago: University of Chicago Press, 1960), 26–47.

have summarized above? For example, suppose that he had described Marbury's attempts to prove his case and had written the following:

> Marbury asked for affidavits from the secretary of state's office, but was refused. He asked the Senate for certified extracts from its minutes, but was refused. Witnesses did not come voluntarily, but had to be subpoenaed. Once the witnesses were at court, they objected to testifying until they were ordered to testify. Their testimony was vague, but the most probable inference is that Marbury's commission was signed, sealed, but not delivered. The secretary of state has refused to appear in court; nor has the secretary of state filed any pleadings; nor has the attorney general appeared to argue the case. Since the defendant, the secretary of state, has not contested the factual allegations, we must assume the plaintiff's allegations are true. The question before the court is whether a default judgment should be entered against the defendant because of his failure to defend.

My own judgment is that Marshall's opinion would have been unpersuasive, if it had begun in this way. Such a stark beginning would have made transparent what the actual opinion in fact concealed, namely, Marshall's political incentive for finding that he had no jurisdiction. If the political incentives had been so clearly exposed, then it would be hard to keep a straight face while reading the legal analysis of the court's lack of jurisdiction. It would have provoked our latent cynicism. Had Marshall written my imaginary paragraph, the political context of the case would have been brought into the foreground, and we would have been inclined to make a political analysis of Marshall's opinion. Furthermore, the beginning that I have imagined would have disrupted the linguistic unity of Marshall's opinion. Marshall's own opinion, unblemished by my crude prose, flows smoothly and seamlessly. He writes with confidence, with precision, with power. But the beginning I have imagined evokes frustration, doubt, and failure. How could he have managed the transition? How could he have moved from frustration to confidence?

Perhaps I can now return to Marshall's first two sentences and explain their significance. Recall that Marshall began:

> At the last term on the affidavits then read and filed with the clerk, a rule was granted in this case, requiring the secretary of state to

show cause why a mandamus should not issue, directing him to deliver to William Marbury his commission as a justice of the peace for the county of Washington, in the district of Columbia.

No cause has been shown, and the present motion is for a mandamus. (*Marbury*, 153–54)

I would now like to suggest that these two sentences lure us into Marshall's legal universe, just as the phrase "once upon a time" can lure us into the world of make-believe and fairy tale. These words are so calmly legal that they seduce us into believing that the world can be described with legal language. This awesome claim—that one can describe our world with legal vocabulary—is Marshall's most fundamental legal fiction, and once we grant it, he has won.

But wait! How can I call this a "fiction"? As I have already said, the world can be described in many different ways, and all of them can be legitimate. Furthermore, I previously alluded to the popular understanding of the word "fiction" as being "a story about something that didn't really happen." However, what Marshall says happened did in fact happen: affidavits were filed, an order to show cause was issued, no cause was shown, and so forth. Isn't all of that *true*? Yes and No.

Yes, several different alternative descriptions could all be true, and thus, Marshall utters truths when he writes that affidavits were filed, that an order was issued, and so forth. However, there is a danger that can be overlooked. Suppose that a description is proclaimed as the sole possible description, and suppose further that the one who describes begins to believe that the words spoken (or written) are the only way, the natural way (the best way, the authoritative way), to speak about the world. This claim is false. Recall that in Chapter 1 I argued that the decision to include some facts while omitting others could yield a story that was misleading, and thus false. The example that I used was an employee who was fired, who had made speeches critical of the boss, and who had had fights with his coworker; to omit either the speeches or the fights is to mislead. I repeat here what I stated in Chapter 1: the ratio of fact to fiction in a story does not correspond to the ratio of truth to falsehood in that story. One may (although one need not, for there is no logical compulsion in the judgment of how much omitting is too much) judge Marshall's selective omissions of the facts to have generated a story that is misleading. But we should not accuse him of lying, since he is totally sincere. Marshall, I believe, writes with deep moral passion.[10] If he deceives us, it is only because he has first deceived himself.[11]

Persuasion in this case depends on the fiction that the legal description is the most authoritative. As I hope I have shown above, if Marshall had included in his opinion a description of its political context, his legal analysis of jurisdiction would strike us as merely clever, as merely an ingenious way to avoid the real difficulties of the case. Indeed, we would question his good faith, his sincerity, his motives for writing as he does. But so far as I know, students (and, I suspect, most law professors) do not have this response. It seems as though most of us quite willingly take Marshall's opinion at face value.

III

The secret power of Marshall's opinion flows from the consistent tone of his discourse. His opening paragraphs describe the history of the case in legal terminology, and the remainder of the opinion, so far as it is possible to do so, stays within this world of legal discourse. To be sure, the world outside does intrude, but Marshall succeeds, to an extraordinary degree, in maintaining the integrity of his discourse. For example, Marshall begins his analysis of the issues before him with the issue that is easiest to describe in legal terms. Recall that Marshall dismisses the case on the grounds that he has no jurisdiction over it, and purists have noted that a strict adherence to propriety would have required him to limit his opinion to the jurisdictional issue.[12] Indeed, his successors in the judiciary have noted that most of the opinion is technically mere dictum,[13] and thus irrelevant to the jurisdictional issue. However, those who argue the purist's thesis have generally ignored the rhetorical advantages of Marshall's strategy. He asserted that the first question was, "Has the applicant a right to the commission he demands?" (*Marbury*, 154). I agree that the ensuing analysis is irrelevant, and

10. See my remarks about Justice Hugo Black in Chapter 1 on page 21.

11. See Herbert Fingarette, *Self-Deception* (London: Routledge & Kegan Paul, 1969).

12. See William W. Van Alstyne, "A Critical Guide to *Marbury v. Madison*," 1969 *Duke L. J.* 1.

13. For instances, see the list of cases in the notes to page 12 of *Constitutional Law*, ed. Paul A. Freund, Arthur E. Sutherland, Mark DeWolfe Howe, and Ernest J. Brown (Boston: Little, Brown, 1967).

thus dictum, if he has no jurisdiction to discuss the merits of the case. But this discussion—the right to the commission—has the advantage of beginning with a topic that looks traditionally legal.

In setting up this first question, Marshall quotes from the congressional act providing for justices of the peace in the District of Columbia, from the constitutional provision providing for appointment of "officers of the United States," from the constitutional provision for the commissioning of such officers, and from the congressional act regulating the secretary of state's responsibility to affix the seal of the United States to commissions. We can see Marshall's true genius at work if we notice how he uses these quotations. He does not declare that these legal texts are authoritative; he assumes their authority without declaring it, then lifts from these texts a vocabulary, which he uses as though it were complete and exhaustive. As Marshall puts it: "They [the congressional acts and the Constitution] seem to contemplate three distinct operations: . . . nomination . . . appointment . . . commission. . ." (155–56). And he then proceeds to redescribe the events in this language (156–59). (Perhaps I should point out that Marshall's use of the constitutional language as his terms of description might be condemned as unprofessional by modern standards. For example, Henry M. Hart and Albert M. Sacks state that the two processes of declaring law and identifying the facts should employ distinct vocabularies: "It will be observed that if this job [of fact identification] is to be done as a distinct one, without question-begging, the relevant characteristics [of the facts] must be identified without using any of the terms used in the general proposition [of law] to be applied. . . . This is a cardinal principle of lawyerlike fact-finding."[14]

When Marshall accepts the legal language—"appointment" and "commission"—as descriptive language, and when he goes further and acts as though (but never says) that it is the only imaginable language for describing, he is well on his way to constructing a fictional world. He also takes another step and assumes that his descriptive labels—appointment and commission—are dichotomous. Marshall declares that appointing an office and commissioning an officer are two sharply different actions. (*Marbury*, 156–62). The president appoints by signing his name to the official document that we call (somewhat confusingly) "the commission." The secretary of state then commissions by affixing the great seal of the United States to the document, recording it in the official records of the department and delivering it to the

14. Henry M. Hart Jr. and Albert M. Sacks, *The Legal Process: Basic Problems in the Making and Application of Law* (Cambridge, Mass.: multilithed, 1958), 375.

officer.[15] This dichotomizing need not be objectionable; sometimes it is convenient. However, Marshall does not separate the two so sharply for reasons of mere convenience.

Marshall uses the distinction between appointing and commissioning to separate the realms of politics and law. The act of appointing is the president's, and concerning it his judgment and will is final, but the process of commissioning is governed by law. If Marshall can make this distinction plausible, then he can gain enormous rhetorical advantage from the distinction. If the distinction is plausible here (and it surely is), then we may be lulled into believing that it will be plausible everywhere (which it isn't). Note how economically and elegantly Marshall builds great consequences on this distinction:

> The commission being signed, the subsequent duty of the secretary of state is prescribed by law, and not to be guided by the will of the President. He is to affix the seal of the United States to the commission, and is to record it.
>
> This is not a proceeding which may be varied, if the judgment of the executive shall suggest one more eligible; but is a precise course accurately marked out by law, and is to be strictly pursued. It is the duty of the secretary of state to conform to the law, and in this he is an officer of the United States, bound to obey the laws. He acts, in this respect, as has been very properly stated at the bar, under the authority of law, and not by instructions of the President. It is a ministerial act which the law enjoins on a particular officer for a particular purpose. (*Marbury*, 158).

I have quoted these two paragraphs because they illustrate so well Marshall's characteristic style in *Marbury*, and furthermore, how his discussion of this "irrelevant" issue (recall that the point is dictum, if there is no jurisdiction) foreshadows the discussion of judicial review. In this context, Marshall describes two alternatives: the secretary of state can conform to "the precise course accurately marked out by the law"; or he can conform to the "will" and "instructions" of the president. As we shall see, similar dichotomies are erected in his discourse on judicial review.

Throughout this first part of the opinion (154–62), Marshall has been

---

15. Of course, these acts need not be done personally by the secretary; subordinate clerks can do the physical acts.

answering his first question, namely, whether Marbury has a right to the commission, even though it had not been delivered to him. I have not discussed the bulk of these eight pages, but the above should be sufficient to show how Marshall begins the work of persuading. Let us now look at the second part of the opinion: "This brings us to the second enquiry; which is, 2ndly. If he has a right, and that right has been violated, do the laws of his country afford him a remedy?" (162).

As the reader might well imagine by now, Marshall will take high ground in answering this question. The two sentences which follow immediately after the question are a fine specimen of his elevated prose: "The very essence of civil liberty certainly consists in the right of every individual to claim the protection of the laws, whenever he receives an injury. One of the first duties of government is to afford that protection" (163). On reading, one nods yes, as perhaps one should, for were these sentences to stand alone, or in another context, one could and should assent. But once again, I caution that one can state the truth without stating the whole truth, and further, the assertion of a partial truth as though it were the whole truth leads one into the realm of fiction.

It is certainly true that one cannot enjoy "the Blessings of Liberty" unless one's liberty is protected by government, and furthermore, access to the judicial process is one of the techniques of protection. However, an honest and impartial police are also a prerequisite to liberty, and the judges do not have the power to give us a police force that respects our liberty. Indeed, unless the executive "shall take care that the laws be faithfully executed," we cannot have liberty, and of course, the judiciary cannot do much to hold the executive to its task. The legislature, the press, and the public have a far more powerful impact on executive rectitude than the judiciary does.[16] Moreover, the legislature and the executive have much to do in order to put in place the prerequisites for liberty. As the Preamble to the Constitution puts it, we must also "insure domestic Tranquility, provide for the common defense, [and] promote the general Welfare" so that we can "secure the Blessings of Liberty to ourselves and our Posterity."

In the last paragraph, I have tried to lure the reader into understanding the larger political context of liberty, and thus, to suggest that one need not stay within the limits of Marshall's discourse. However, even if one stays within the world of Marshall's discourse, there is a problem; the real problem

16. See, for example, Arthur M. Schlesinger Jr., *The Imperial Presidency* (Boston: Houghton Mifflin, 1973).

with the second question is that it does not sound like much of a question. The answer seems so obvious and so easy that there does not seem to be much to say about it. Indeed, the question as posed suggests a logical impossibility, for "if the laws furnish no remedy for the violation of a vested right" (*Marbury*, 163), then one does not have a properly functioning legal system in place. Or else, the words "laws" and "remedy" and "vested rights" are being used in a rather strange way. The question is so peculiar that one is puzzled; or as Marshall responds to his own question: "If this obloquy [that the laws furnish no remedy for the violation of a right] is to be cast on the jurisprudence of our country, it must arise from the peculiar character of the case."

We turn, then, to the "peculiar character" of this particular case to ask whether there is something unique about it. One possibility that Marshall addresses is that this case might be one to which the maxim *damnum absque injuria* might be applicable. In other words, one might have the violation of a right (the *damnum*) without there being the type of injury (the *injuria*) the law deems worthy of recognition. However, Marshall quite properly rejects this possibility. It would be wrong to say that Marbury has only suffered some sort of trivial psychic injury, which a sturdy legal system should dismiss with a gruff, no-nonsense snort. Marshall notes that Marbury is seeking something that is far from being worthless; he is seeking an office of "trust . . . honor . . . [and] profit" (164). (If I understand the context of this remark correctly, I interpret Marshall as suggesting that a justice of the peace enjoys *trust* and *honor* because of social esteem and he enjoys *profit* because of the fees he charges.) Consequently, Marshall dismisses abruptly, as well he should, the relevance of *damnum absque injuria*.

What other grounds might there be for saying that the right might not have a remedy? Marshall suggests that perhaps there might be something about "the nature of the transaction" (164) that might take it outside the realm of judicial remedies. For example, it might be "a mere political act, belonging to the executive department alone." Marshall quickly concedes that there are such cases, and thus, that there are some executive acts that may not be reexamined by judges. But not all executive acts are immune from judicial scrutiny; so how do we tell them apart? Marshall's response is "If some acts be examinable, and others not, there must be some rule of law to guide the court in the exercise of its jurisdiction" (165).

I have been puzzled for many years by this sentence. It strikes me as being an important step in Marshall's argument, but I find it hard to interpret and suspect that its ambiguity is part of its power. An extreme reading of the sentence would be that legal language has the power to state how one should draw the line between law and politics. I call this reading extreme, since to read the sentence this way is to make extraordinary claims on behalf of legal language. If the professional vocabulary of judges can describe powerfully and adequately the difference between law and politics, then judges command rich and resourceful idiom. One ought to doubt. Would not some third idiom, perhaps drawn from philosophy or history, be necessary? If we are to say that a particular transaction is within the jurisdiction of law (and thus the judiciary) or of politics (and thus the executive), where can we find a place to stand to discern where the case should be? To look for the line with legal optics (or with the glass of politics) is to prejudge the boundary.

However, we need not impute extreme views to Marshall, for it may be that he wishes to assert a far more modest point. He could be acknowledging that judges are not experts in philosophy and history, that once judges leave behind their professional learning then they have no claim to know more than others do, and that consequently, the line must be drawn by way of a legal rule, or else judges will be incompetent to draw it. Of course, it would be preferable to have a neutral idiom for drawing the line between executive jurisdiction and judicial jurisdiction, but judges must judge by way of law. As I have said, I am inclined to attribute the more modest claim to Marshall, but my experience in teaching this case is that students tend to read this passage more broadly.[17] Students often feel that there is no problem whatsoever—why of course the line can be drawn by a legal rule! To the extent that students fail to discern a problem, Marshall has succeeded. The earlier passages have made the legal vocabulary seem natural and inevitable.

At any rate, Marshall investigates the drawing of the much-needed line by reading the Constitution and the statutes of the United States, and he finds his answer in those texts. He starts with the Constitution and notes that it grants to the president "certain important political powers" and that the president's "discretion" in exercising these powers is to be reviewed politically, not judicially (*Marbury*, 165–66). One should note that the Constitution does not describe the president's powers as being "political," and furthermore, the document certainly doesn't declare that "the political" and "the legal" are dichotomous spheres. This interpretive move—the claim

17. Of course, I do not necessarily discuss this point, since the students quite often become interested in other issues, and thus the vagaries of time keep me away from it. Consequently, that sample of occasions in which I have been struck by the way students read this passage may not in fact be typical.

that presidential powers can be classified as "political"—is the first step toward Marshall's line-drawing. But to make the interpretation practical, he goes on to note that the president does not exercise his powers without aid; indeed, Marshall observes that the Constitution authorizes the president to appoint officers to help him carry out his responsibilities. And if the president can appoint officers to do his political work, then their doing of this political work can only be reviewed politically (165–66).

However—there is always a "however"—these officers do not always act solely on behalf of the president. The Congress may pass statutes that impose nonpolitical duties on those whom the president has appointed. One should pause and savor the brilliance of this "however." Marshall is now restating, at a higher level of abstraction, an assumption implicit in all that has gone before, and I think that he persuades because of the subtle repetition with variation in his argument. As he now recapitulates what has gone before, he characterizes the secretary of state as someone with two loyalties and two sources of authority, the Congress and the president.

Marshall summarizes his analysis in the following splendid example of his characteristic prose:

> The conclusion from this reasoning is, that where the heads of departments are the political or confidential agents of the executive, merely to execute the will of the President, or rather to act in cases in which the executive possesses a constitutional or legal discretion, nothing can be more perfectly clear than that their acts are only politically examinable. But where a specific duty is assigned by law, and individual rights depend upon the performance of that duty, it seems equally clear that the individual who considers himself injured, has a right to resort to the laws of his country for a remedy. (166)

This impressive prose has a dual appeal: it rests on a complicated truth; it promises a clean solution to the complication. The truth is that the secretary of state *does* have two loyalties. It is surely right to say that a president can require the secretary of state to execute the president's foreign policy, not that of someone else; and it is also correct to say that a Congress can impose legal duties on a secretary of state; and so John Marshall speaks truly in recognizing the dual authority of Congress and the president. The complication is that this dual authority of Congress and president can make life miserable for a secretary of state. John Marshall's fiction is that he has a clean and simple solution to the complicated misery of dual loyalty. Marshall's thesis is that one can read the Constitution and our statutes and discern exactly where discretion leaves off and duty begins. We are tempted to believe him because we desire a solution so strongly.

The upshot of the above is that Marshall concludes that there is nothing peculiar or distinctive about this "transaction" and thus that Marbury has a remedy. Marshall is now ready to move to part 3 of this opinion. In part 1, he concluded that Marbury had been deprived of a right; in part 2, that the laws provide a remedy for this deprivation; in part 3 (168–76), he will address procedural questions; Did Marbury file the right sort of pleading? Did he file it in the right court?

The question of whether Marbury filed the right sort of pleading is more typical of Marshall's day than of our own. In those days, lawyers had to learn a system known as "common law pleading." Even today, lawyers are responsible for constructing a sound legal theory in support of their clients' cases; in those days, one also was responsible for knowing which "writ" had to be used for asserting the several different legal theories. Furthermore, a mistake—putting the right legal theory into the wrong writ—was a serious matter; a mismatch between theory and writ would lead to a dismissal of the case. However, Charles Lee had done a good job, and Marshall quite correctly held that the right pleading was used.[18]

If the proper pleading was used, was it filed in the proper court? As most know, Marshall's justly famous answer to this question was—No! If we do not inflate it too much, this "No" seems both proper and unremarkable. After all, the Constitution instructs each branch of government on how it should do its job. Consequently, if the president were to call on the Congress to abandon the law-making procedures that are specified in the document (for example, if the House of Representatives and the Senate were urged to sit as a single assembly), then the Congress should refuse. So too, if the Congress made an analogous call on the chief executive (for example, if the Congress urged the president to submit all major decisions to the cabinet before acting), the president should refuse. Therefore, it was surely appropriate for the justices of the Supreme Court to assert a jurisdiction that the Constitution does not authorize. Of course, there are some technical questions that Marshall had to address. Did the Judiciary Act give the Supreme Court jurisdiction over Marbury's case? If so, was this grant in excess of the constitutional grant of jurisdiction? To answer these questions, Marshall had

18. *Marbury*, 168–73. "Mandamus" was the right writ for calling on a public officer to perform a legal duty.

to interpret the relevant documents—section 13 of the Judiciary Act of 1789, and Article III, Section 2, of the Constitution—and his interpretation of these documents has *not* been universally praised.[19] The difficulties in interpreting the documents stem partly from the technicalities of "original" versus "appellate" jurisdiction (and I refer the reader to Van Alstyne's "Critical Guide") and partly from disagreements among scholars about the history of those two documents and about what the drafters were trying to do. For what it may be worth, I happen to believe that Marshall got the technicalities wrong, but I hasten to add that his reading of these technical matters is completely reasonable. I happen to differ, but I certainly don't believe that Marshall was unreasonable in resolving these questions the way he did.

At any rate, the case is not famous because of the arcane topic of jurisdiction. The importance of *Marbury* rests on the rhetoric that Marshall uses. Marshall does not merely justify the self-restraint of saying no. He seems to go further, and in going further, he shaped the way many have thought about the Constitution. Marshall begins his famous discussion of constitutional theory quite modestly. He states: "The authority, therefore, given to the supreme court, by the act establishing the judicial courts of the United States, to issue writs of mandamus to public officers, appears not to be warranted by the constitution; and it becomes necessary to inquire whether a jurisdiction, so conferred, can be exercised" (*Marbury*, 176). This passage states the issue quite modestly; it asks no more than whether the Supreme Court can exercise a statutory power that is beyond its constitutional power. However, Marshall rather quickly goes beyond this statement of the issue and asserts that the question is "whether an act, repugnant to the constitution, can become the law of the land. . . ." (176).

We can quibble with this statement, although my main point is somewhat different. The quibble is that this statement is too abstract and unclear. It is unclear because it is obscure whether it adds anything to what has gone before. For example, it is possible that an act of Congress could be part of the law of the land, but only imperfectly so, in that certain powers granted by the act cannot be exercised by those to whom the powers are granted. There need be no all-or-nothing answers to whether an act is part of "the law of the land." (Consider all of the practical problems that arise when someone relies on a statute and acts in accordance with the statute, and then the statute is held unconstitutional. There are no simple answers to such problems.) However, this is merely a quibble about the logic of the sentence; I think it more important to attend to the rhetoric of the sentence.

19. See Van Alstyne, "A Critical Guide to *Marbury v. Madison*," 1.

The rhetoric of this sentence collocates "the constitution" and "the law" and thus sets the theme for the next three pages of Marshall's opinion, three pages in which this collocation becomes an identity, three pages in which the judiciary's power to decide cases becomes the power to declare the law, which in turn becomes a power to speak in the voice of the Constitution. To be sure, "the Constitution" and "the law" are not discrete categories. They are connected; they intertwine; it would be a gross distortion to separate them. But it also seems simplistic to collapse the two; however, Marshall's opinion has had the effect of preparing the reader for this identification of the Constitution and the law for many pages.

Recall that he described the history of the case and the conduct of the president and the secretary of state in legal terms. Furthermore, the very structure of the opinion, the sequence of topics—does Marbury have a right, was the right violated, is there a remedy for the violation, has the right writ been used to seek the remedy, has the writ been filed in the proper court—this very ordering of the questions presupposes that legal categories are the appropriate categories of analysis. We are now prepared for legal analysis to capture the Constitution, although even John Marshall will have to transcend legal analysis to carry this off.

In this powerful finale, Marshall goes outside the law to political theory and history. He bows toward "the people," saying that they have authority to erect whatever form of government they wish. We all nod, Yes. Marshall also declares that this supreme power cannot be frequently exercised, nor should it. Well, one might want to hedge a bit; Jefferson thought that regularly scheduled exercises of the supreme power would be a good idea; but Madison thought the proposal was daft, and so Marshall may be right on grounds of practicality. [20] At any rate, Marshall has pushed the analysis back to the source of supreme authority, and he need only ask what that authority has done. In asking what "the people" have done, Marshall notes that there are only two things they could have done (another dichotomy): "This original and supreme will organizes the government, and assigns, to different departments, their respective powers. It may either stop here; or establish certain limits not to be transcended by those departments" (176). One could quibble; a grant also implies a limit; when agents act outside the scope of their grant, they have exceeded the limits of their power. Still, Marshall is surely right that our Constitution does contain sentences that read as though they were meant to "establish . . . limits." If there are limits, who shall enforce them?

20. Garry Wills, *Inventing America* (Garden City, N.Y.: Doubleday, 1978), 125–28.

The Constitution itself does not say. Note that the president has the power to veto legislation. This power is specifically mentioned, and if it had not been mentioned, no one would have supposed that the president would enjoy such an extraordinary power. However, the Constitution does not say that judges have the power to veto legislation. Such a power is also extraordinary; should we not say that the Constitution's silence on this topic is significant?[21] Indeed, it is true that the ordinary rules of legal exegesis would lead one to say that the judiciary has no veto power, since extraordinary powers do not exist unless they are specifically granted; however, the problem is an extraordinary one and thus is not covered by ordinary rules. To solve an extraordinary problem one has to return to first principles.

In considering the matter of how limits can best be enforced, Marshall was caught in a difficult position: he couldn't use the best argument, namely, the one that makes the most sense in terms of practical politics. As a practical matter, what is the best way of enforcing the limits? The judiciary, as compared to the legislature and executive, is relatively detached from the daily affairs of politics. Furthermore, the judiciary, unlike "the people," is relatively well organized. Consequently, one can combine these two observations—that the judiciary is relatively detached and relatively well organized—and assign it the job by default. To be sure, one could argue that unless the job can be done perfectly, it shouldn't be done at all; but one might instead prefer the golden maxim of G. K. Chesterton: "If a job is worth doing, it is worth doing badly." The only practical question is, What is the least bad way of doing it?

Unfortunately, John Marshall could not make this eminently practical argument—the tone is all wrong. I tried to write the preceding paragraph to give it a no-nonsense tone that would seem slightly crude, perhaps even flip. And of course, my flippancy falls miles short of the elevated tone that characterizes Marshall's prose. But perhaps what I have said could be polished. The basic thesis is that we need to know the "least bad" way of doing a job, which entails that we need to speculate on the relative capacity of those who might do it. One could dress up talk about "relative capacity" with some impressive jargon, but even so, there would be a problem. Marshall could not have made the "relative capacity" argument because of the political context within which he wrote. The Federalist party (Marshall's party) has just been rejected at the polls by the new Jeffersonian party known

---

21. George Anastaplo, *The Constitution of 1787* (Baltimore: Johns Hopkins University Press, 1989), 47–48, 139–45.

as the Republicans. Marshall himself is a rookie judge who took office by way of the shabby maneuvers of lame duck politicians. Marshall could not argue that a Federalist judiciary was more worthy of the people's trust than a Jeffersonian legislature and executive. Consequently, Marshall needed to avoid the "who" and focus on the "what," namely, he had to state the issue as impersonally and abstractly as possible.

Marshall puts it as follows:

> The distinction, between a government with limited and unlimited powers, is abolished, if those limits do not confine the persons on whom they are imposed, and if acts prohibited and acts allowed, are of equal obligation. It is a proposition too plain to be contested, that the constitution controls any legislative act repugnant to it; or,that the legislature may alter the constitution by an ordinary act.
>
> Between these alternatives there is no middle ground. The constitution is either a superior, paramount law, unchangeable by ordinary means, or it is on a level with ordinary legislative acts, and like other acts, is alterable when the legislature shall please to alter it. (*Marbury*, 176–77)

Recall that Marshall had previously drawn a contrast between "law" and "politics" in terms of the "precise course" of the law versus the "discretion" of political actors. This prior theme of "duty and right" versus "will and discretion" is now extended to the Constitution itself, which is to be "a superior, paramount law," and thus can presumably prescribe a "precise course" and a realm of "duty and right." One should pause and admire. With this rhetorical flourish, Marshall has bequeathed to his successors a story about the law that they can tell—the story that law in general, constitutional law in particular, is above politics, is not subject to political whim. Like most significant stories, it can be told to do good or to do ill.

Of course, the logic of the story has some weak places, although it may seem churlish of me to ruin a good story with mere logic. Consider Marshall's sentence

> It is a proposition too plain to be contested, that the constitution controls any *legislative act* repugnant to it; or, that the *legislature* may alter the constitution by an ordinary act" (177, emphasis added).

Now consider my rewrite:

It is a proposition too plain to be contested, that the constitution controls any *judicial decision* repugnant to it; or, that the *supreme court* may alter the constitution by an ordinary act.

In other words, whoever has the final say can change the Constitution. Marshall would have us believe that the Constitution is "a superior, paramount law, unchangeable by ordinary means." But his argument (viewed through the cruel microscope of logic) does not yield this conclusion. If we grant John Marshall the power to veto an act of Congress, then indeed it will follow that the judiciary can prevent the Congress from changing the Constitution by the ordinary act of passing a statute. It will also follow that the Supreme Court will have this terrible power, since the Supreme Court can now change the Constitution by the ordinary act of deciding a case. (And by the way, they have done it.)

However, the logical flaw in Marshall's argument does not detract from the importance of what Marshall is saying. Stability in the law is important to us. We would all like to believe that we have certain rights that no one can take away from us. Marshall may not have a perfect answer, but he is talking about an important question. Do we have rights that no one can take away from us? Do we have rights that are not subject to the vagaries of political whim? Is there a "precise course of law" that marks off where we can safely stand? I do not wish to answer these questions either yes or no, even though I do have an opinion, and even though my opinion is on the cynical side. What I do wish to assert is that most of my fellow citizens and I share a culture in which the answer is yes. Even when people understand that the answer might be no, they believe that the answer ought *not* be no, it ought to be yes. This belief, this hope, is powerful, yet perhaps also fragile.

What story, then, can be told that can feed the flames of this desire? John Marshall has shown us how to tell a story in which "law" is other than "politics," and he has shown us the story must be told using the right words, not the wrong words. If the story can be told with legal words, and if those words can be made to seem natural, inevitable, accurate—indeed, the only possible words—then perhaps we can believe in law. However, a caveat. Although I honor the power of Marshall's legal discourse, there is linguistic evidence that this discourse is vulnerable. Our evidence is that the word "legalistic" is a curse, whereas the word "lawful" is a eulogy. But what is the difference between the "legalistic" and the "lawful"? *Marbury* does not give us a story that will answer this question.

3

The Story of Growth

Marshall's most famous opinion, after *Marbury v. Madison*, is *McCulloch v. Maryland*.[1] The *McCulloch* opinion contrasts sharply with *Marbury* in that it confronts the world of change. In *Marbury*, Marshall speaks within the discourse of legalism; in *McCulloch*, he doesn't.

1

We can discern the contrast between *Marbury* and *McCulloch* by comparing their first paragraphs. The case began when representatives of the State of

---

1. 4 Wheaton 316 (1819).

Maryland sued a representative of the Bank of the United States. Congress had chartered the Bank of the United States, and the directors of the bank had in turn established a branch in Baltimore; McCulloch was in charge of the Baltimore branch. Maryland had passed an act imposing taxes on any bank not chartered by the Maryland legislature that issued bank notes within the State. (The tax was an "excise tax," or what one might call a "transaction tax," analogous to the modern sales tax. In modern times, eating a meal in a restaurant, buying a suit in a department store, or attending a major league baseball game are quite commonly taxable transactions. The Maryland statute was analogous. According to the Maryland statute, the issuing of banknotes, if done by a bank that was not chartered by the state, was a taxable event.) Since the Bank of the United States was not chartered by Maryland (but by Congress) and since the Baltimore branch of the bank issued banknotes, it followed that McCulloch (who was in charge of the Baltimore branch) was duty bound (if the Maryland statute was valid) to pay the tax. Consequently, Maryland sued McCulloch in the state court, and he lost. McCulloch took his case to the Supreme Court by way of a procedure that no longer exists, "the writ of error," and so in accordance with the practice in 1819, the date of the Supreme Court opinion, McCulloch was the "plaintiff in error" and Maryland the "defendant in error." In the paragraph that I shall now quote, Marshall abbreviates this customary designation, referring to McCulloch as "plaintiff" and to Maryland as "defendant."

Note how Marshall begins by highlighting the political contest behind the case. In *Marbury*, Marshall wrote in a way that disguised the confrontation between a lame duck Federalist judiciary and the newly elected Jeffersonian legislature and executive. In *McCulloch*, however, he emphasizes the political contest between state and nation.

> In the case now to be determined, the defendant, a sovereign State, denies the obligation of a law enacted by the legislature of the Union, and the plaintiff, on his part, contests the validity of an act which has been passed by the legislature of that State. The constitution of our country, in its most interesting and vital parts, is to be considered; the conflicting powers of the government of the Union and of its members, as marked in that constitution, are to be discussed; and an opinion given, which may essentially influence the great operations of the government. No tribunal can approach such a question without a deep sense of its importance, and of the awful responsibility involved in its decision. But it must be decided peacefully, or remain

a source of hostile legislation, perhaps of hostility of a still more serious nature; and if it is to be so decided, by this tribunal alone can the decision be made. On the Supreme Court of the United States has the constitution of our country devolved this important duty. (*McCulloch*, 400–401)

I would like to emphasize the sequence of topics in the five sentences which constitute this paragraph in order to highlight an important claim that Marshall is advancing. My restating of this sequence will inevitably flatten out the rhythms of Marshall's prose, which is regrettable. The sequence of the five sentences is as follows. First, there is a conflict in which the parties are denying the validity of legislative acts and thus the conflict between the parties becomes in turn a conflict between state and union. Second, this conflict entails that the "vital parts" of the Constitution must be "considered" and "discussed." Third, deciding these issues is declared to be an "awful responsibility." Fourth, there is a need for a peaceful resolution of the conflict, or else the failure to have a peaceful resolution will lead to "hostile legislation," resolution, or if not that, something even more serious, "perhaps of hostility of a still more serious nature" (war?). And, fifth, the Supreme Court has the duty to resolve the dispute peacefully.

This sequence of topics sets the stage for the opinion that follows with dramatic, indeed almost portentous, flourish. In *Marbury*, Marshall began with a dry legal discourse that took the drama out of the dispute; here, he begins as dramatically as he can. In *Marbury*, Marshall sought authority by removing himself from the sphere of politics; but here in *McCulloch*, he seeks authority by injecting himself into the middle of the conflict.

It is most remarkable that both opinions, despite their different styles, work, that is, they both persuade. In both, Marshall claims authority on behalf of the judiciary, and each claim persuades us because each appeals to a fundamental desire. In *Marbury*, we desire the security of rights, a realm of rules and reason not subject to destruction by political will. Here in *McCulloch*, we desire something rather different. The world of *McCulloch* is a Hobbesian world of political conflict, which is potentially a world of political violence, and in this world only the judiciary can secure peace.

Of course, Marshall's claim that peace depends on judges is hyperbole. But is it a fiction? The word "fiction" is not a precise term; consequently, the question does not have a precise answer. I want to say yes—Marshall is writing fiction, rather than a false theory, when he asserts that only the Supreme Court can deliver peace—but my yes is fuzzy and qualified.

One of my problems is that Marshall's assertion is so brief that it can strike one as a "theory" rather than as a "story." For example, one might interpret Marshall's paragraph as asserting an abstract thesis such as the following—whenever there is a conflict between national legislative power and state legislative power, neither the legislature nor the executive can resolve it peacefully, only the judiciary can. Alternatively, one can interpret the paragraph as presenting a drama, a story—the Congress acted, then the Maryland legislature responded, but McCulloch honored only what Congress did, so Maryland sued, and the state court held for the state, and thus we now have a terrible conflict, which Congress cannot resolve, which the president cannot resolve, which only the Supreme Court can resolve. Both of these interpretations are plausible. Indeed, I would say that both of them are "right," and furthermore, that this duality is part of the "secret," that this duality makes the paragraph more persuasive than it would otherwise be. We yearn for both stories and theories, and Marshall gives us both.

Both interpretations—the paragraph is both "theory" and "story"—fit the textual facts. On the one hand, Marshall's prose is abstract, just as theories are abstract. On the other hand, the prose presents a dramatic sequence of events, just as stories do. Since the paragraph has the dual aspect of story and theory, I certainly cannot object to anyone who wishes to focus on the theoretical side of *McCulloch*. However, I wish to focus on the narrative. If we focus on the narrative in *McCulloch*, we can ask the questions that we normally ask about stories: Who is the hero? What does the hero do? Why is the hero a hero? Two of these questions are easy to answer: the judges are the heroes, and they are heroes because they bring peace. But it is harder to say what judges do that differs from what other heroes do. The judges interpret the Constitution, but so does everyone else. How do judges interpret? Do they do it differently? If I read Marshall correctly, judges are different because they act under the compulsion of duty. The members of the Supreme Court did not leave their chambers and go out to search for this case; the parties brought it to them. They must now decide the case because "the constitution of our country [has] devolved this important duty" upon them. This description contains an implied but unstated contrast. The contrast is that legislators, unlike judges, decide matters because they want to. In short, judges are trustworthy because they act from duty, not desire.

This story—that judges stand above the fray and thus can bring peace—is largely fictional. Consider, for example, the divisions that led to the Civil War. David Morris Potter and Don E. Fehrenbacher have written excellent studies of these events, and their accounts lead me to believe that the story of neutral judges bringing peace is indeed a fiction.[2] In the antebellum era, judges were no more detached from the passions of their time than were other public figures. Furthermore, judicial decisions had no more calming effect on the populace than did legislative decisions. However, like other fictional stories that judges tell, this story about bringing peace is not told dishonestly, then or now. It is believed. Robert A. Burt has shown how this belief—that judges can impose peace—is still alive and how it captures the judicial imagination in our own time.[3] Burt also believes that the story is dangerous, since imposing "peace" can generate dangerous resentments. I do not wish to generalize about the possible dangers; I merely wish to point out that there is a story here, and that it is fictional.

Marshall's *McCulloch* opinion is thirty-seven pages long, but not all of it has been equally influential. The second part of the opinion, in which Marshall discusses Maryland's lack of power to tax the bank, has been less influential than the first part, in which he discusses Congress's power to establish the bank. In the second part, Marshall starts off with sweeping generalities that almost lead one to believe that the state cannot tax a federal bank simply because it is a national institution. However, in the very last paragraph, he seems to come down on a rather narrower point, which is, that the Maryland tax is invalid because it interferes with the "operation" of a national institution. This narrow resolution makes most of what has gone before in part 2 seem unnecessary; consequently, it has been less influential, and so I shall limit my discussion to the first part of Marshall's opinion. (*McCulloch*, 400–425).

As Marshall begins his discussion of Congress's power to create the bank, he quite properly notes that the question is not a new one. The issue was hotly debated in the First Congress and in the executive branch.[4] However, the dispute did not go away and the charter of the bank was permitted to expire. But then, five years later (1816), the Congress changed its mind and established the second Bank of the United States, which is the institution being litigated in the case. By 1819, no one who was a member of the national elite seriously doubted the constitutionality of the bank. Marshall's discussion of the history of debate about the bank's constitutionality is rather

2. David Morris Potter, *The Impending Crisis, 1848–1861* (New York: Harper & Row, 1976). Don E. Fehrenbacher, *The Dred Scott Case* (New York: Oxford University Press, 1978).

3. Robert A. Burt, "The Constitution of the Family," 1979 *Sup. Ct. Rev.* 329.

4. For a brief discussion of the legal arguments made in 1791, see Paul Brest and Sanford Levinson, *Processes of Constitutional Decisionmaking*, 3d ed. (Boston: Little, Brown, 1992), 9–17.

abstract. Perhaps Marshall's preference for writing in sweeping generalities is a sufficient explanation for the abstract description. However, I think there are additional reasons. The major political opponents of 1791, Jefferson and Madison, had changed their minds and now conceded that a national bank was constitutional. It would have been bad taste for Marshall to gloat, or to charge inconsistency, and so he put the matter abstractly. His description of how Madison and Jefferson were defeated and then changed their minds has a nice delicacy to it:

> The bill for incorporating the [first] bank of the United States did not steal upon an unsuspecting legislature, and pass unobserved. Its principle was completely understood and was opposed with equal zeal and ability. After being resisted, first in the fair and open field of debate [i.e., Madison], and afterwards in the executive cabinet, with as much persevering talent [i.e., Jefferson] as any measure has ever experienced, and being supported by arguments [i.e., Hamilton] which convinced minds as pure and intelligent as this country can boast [i.e., the first congress and the first president], it became a law. The original act was permitted to expire; but a short experience of the embarrassments to which the refusal to revive it exposed the government, convinced those who were most prejudiced against the measure of its necessity, and induced the passage of the present law. (*McCulloch*, 402)

Marshall next turns to an issue that seems logically irrelevant but rhetorically powerful. The issue is whether the national government gets its powers by way of delegation from the states or from the people. This issue is perhaps logically irrelevant, since in either case the terms of the delegation are supposedly specified in the Constitution. However, it is rather nice to argue, as Marshall does, that both the national government and the state governments are subordinate to the people, as this entails that neither party to the controversy comes to court with a prima facie case to be the origin of power. The origin of power is, according to Marshall's long-standing political theory, the people.

As stated above, this political theory about the people is perhaps irrelevant to the issue—does Congress have power to incorporate a bank? It may be irrelevant because at issue is what power has been granted, and not who granted it. One can argue that the source of the power is irrelevant to the scope of the power.[5] However, I think that it would be a mistake to take such a narrow view of relevance. Under a broader view of relevance, the political theory is relevant in a more subtle way. After all, a strict construction of congressional power might be more persuasive if this power came from the states instead of the people. Unfortunately, this whole debate seems metaphysical, so I suggest that we turn away from the logical question and look at the rhetorical role of Marshall's political theory. Why might Marshall want to say that the people are the ultimate source of power? What persuasive effect does this argument have? And in particular, how does this political theory about the people fit together with the first paragraph of *McCulloch*? Recall that the first paragraph ends with the assertion "it's me or war." (If this claim had been true, it would have been a good reason to give power to Marshall.) Furthermore, there is the implicit claim that Marshall and the judges differ from other political actors because they act under the compulsion of duty, whereas others act from desire. The paragraph of political theory goes well with this first paragraph. By attributing ultimate authority to the people, Marshall is also denying it to other political actors. Furthermore, the people are by definition silent, and so someone must speak in their name. Who? (John Marshall?) I think that Marshall's political theory is a subtle way of weakening the claims of other political actors in order to improve his own. He can bring peace because he speaks in the name of the people, and we can know that he speaks in their name because he only speaks when duty compels.

At any rate, the upshot is clear enough. The national government has powers delegated to it and it may exercise only those powers which have been granted.[6] As Marshall puts it: "This [national] government is acknowledged by all to be one of enumerated powers . . . [and] it can exercise only the powers granted to it. . . . That principle is now universally admitted. But the question respecting the extent of the powers actually granted, is perpetually arising, and will probably continue to arise, as long as our system shall exist" (*McCulloch*, 405).

Assuming that the national government has a power raises a subsidiary logical point. If the national government has a power delegated to it by the Constitution, can that power be "trumped" by state power? Or is the national power always the trump over state power? The question is not difficult;

---

5. See Brest and Levinson, *Processes*, 20n. Let me hasten to add that Brest and Levinson merely raise the argument; they do not assert a conclusion.

6. One might contrast here Marshall's discussion in *Marbury*, in which he suggested that a government of pure grant might be a government without limitations. See chap. 2, n. 21.

national power trumps state power. However, one can establish the point that national power trumps state power in several different ways, and one important feature of Marshall's *McCulloch* opinion is how he establishes the point. Note how he proceeds:

> If any one proposition could command the universal assent of mankind, we might expect it would be this—that the government of the Union, though limited in its powers, is supreme within its sphere of action. This would seem to result necessarily from its nature. It is the government of all; its powers are delegated by all; it represents all, and acts for all. Though any one State may be willing to control its operations, no State is willing to allow others to control them. The nation, on those subjects on which it can act, must necessarily bind its component parts. But this question is not left to mere reason: the people have, in express terms, decided it, by saying, "this constitution, and the laws of the United States, which shall be made in pursuance thereof," "shall be the supreme law of the land." (405–406)

In this passage, Marshall proceeds first by way of an argument from the general nature of the case, and only at the end does he turn to the actual text. This reverses the direction of argument that Marshall used in *Marbury*. Recall that in that case, he drew his basic vocabulary from the text itself, and then proceeded to describe the world with the language drawn therefrom. In *McCulloch*, Marshall starts outside the text, with general principles. G. Edward White has described Marshall's style rather nicely. White states that Marshall's opinion starts with the axioms of political economy, from which he deduces what a good constitution would be like, after which he turns to the text of our own constitution, and he then discovers (surprise! surprise!) that our constitution is a good constitution.[7] A cynic might note that Marshall's technique lets him read into the Constitution his own personal preferences. This is the truth, but not the whole truth. I don't think that Marshall consciously manipulated the text to get a result that he wanted but knew was not authorized. Rather, I think that Marshall's ideas are more deeply held, so that he was not aware of the potential for manipulation, but of

---

7. G. Edward White, *The Marshall Court and Cultural Change, 1815–1835* (New York: Oxford University Press, 1991).

course, I cannot prove this.[8] These psychological questions are hard to answer and, fortunately, not particularly important; what Marshall did is more important than why he did it. What Marshall did was ground his interpretation of the text in a broad vision. (As White puts it, he started with the axioms of political economy.) By resting the text within a broader vision, Marshall integrated constitutional law into the rest of life. In *Marbury*, he isolated the law; in *McCulloch*, he did not.

To be sure, there is a powerful continuity between the two cases. In both, judges do something that differs sharply from what legislature and executive officers do. In both, the implicit claim is that judges should have authority because judges are different. However, the two cases put the difference in different places. In *Marbury*, the judges live in a world of rules where there is no change. In *McCulloch*, the judges live in the world of change and conflict, but they are not moved by the same desires that move others. In both, the world of the law is the world of reason, but the source of reason differs; in one, reason rests on precise rules; in the other, on lofty principles. Unfortunately, both of Marshall's worlds are hard acts to follow; his successors have generally not been as adept as he.

At any rate, Marshall is now six pages into the opinion. He has established that the national government can only exercise those powers which have been delegated to it, but that in exercising these powers, it is supreme over the states. Has the power to charter a bank been delegated? The Constitution is silent; there are no explicit provisions that pronounce either an Aye or a Nay. How, then, will Marshall interpret this silence? How will silence speak? The excerpt that follows is rather long, but it is good, very good; this is Marshall at his best, at his most magisterial and stately:

> Among the enumerated powers, we do not find that of establishing a bank or creating a corporation. But there is no phrase in the instru-

8. I have made my inferences via a literary appraisal of Marshall's prose, namely, by trying to judge what sort of person would write this sort of prose. However, I realize that this literary inference is uncertain. The late Robert Cover warned against simplistic analysis in the following passage: "In a static and simplistic model of law, the judge caught between law and morality has only four choices. He may apply the law against his conscience. He may apply conscience and be faithless to the law. He may resign. Or he may cheat: He may state that the law is not what he believes it to be, and thus preserve an appearance (to others) of conformity of law and morality. Once we assume a more realistic model of law and of the judicial process, these four positions become only poles setting limits to a complex field of action and motive." Robert M. Cover, *Justice Accused: Antislavery and the Judicial Process* (New Haven: Yale University Press, 1975), 6. Cover's thesis, that we not use "a static and simplistic model of law," is also relevant to psychology. We should not use simplistic models of psychology; to accuse Marshall of "manipulation" is to be simplistic.

ment which, like the articles of confederation, excludes incidental or implied powers; and which requires that every thing granted shall be expressly and minutely described. Even the 10th amendment, which was framed for the purpose of quieting the excessive jealousies which had been excited, omits the word "expressly," and declares only that the powers "not delegated to the United States, nor prohibited to the States, are reserved to the States or to the people"; thus leaving the question, whether the particular power which may become the subject of contest has been delegated to the one government, or prohibited to the other, to depend on a fair construction of the whole instrument. The men who drew and adopted this amendment had experienced the embarrassments resulting from the insertion of this word in the articles of confederation, and probably omitted it to avoid those embarrassments. A constitution, to contain an accurate detail of all the subdivisions of which its great powers will admit, and of all the means by which they may be carried into execution, would partake of the prolixity of a legal code, and could scarcely be embraced by the human mind. It would probably never be understood by the public. Its nature, therefore, requires, that only its great outlines should be marked, its important objects designated, and the minor ingredients which compose those objects be deduced from the nature of the objects themselves. That this idea was entertained by the framers of the American constitution, is not only to be inferred from the nature of the instrument, but from the language. Why else were some of the limitations, found in the ninth section of the 1st article, introduced? It is also, in some degree, warranted by their having omitted to use any restrictive term which might prevent its receiving a fair and just interpretation. In considering this question, then, we must never forget, that it is *a constitution* we are expounding.

Although, among the enumerated powers of government, we do not find the word "bank" or "incorporation," we find the great powers to lay and collect taxes; to borrow money; to regulate commerce; to declare and conduct a war; and to raise and support armies and navies. The sword and the purse, all the external relations, and no inconsiderable portion of the industry of the nation, are entrusted to its government. It can never be pretended that these vast powers draw after them others of inferior importance, merely because they are inferior. Such an idea can never be advanced. But it may with great reason be contended, that a government, entrusted with such ample powers, on the due execution of which the happiness and prosperity of the nation so vitally depends, must also be entrusted with ample means for their execution. The power being given, it is the interest of the nation to facilitate its execution. It can never be their interest, and cannot be presumed to have been their intention, to clog and embarrass its executing by withholding the most appropriate means. Throughout this vast republic, from the St. Croix to the Gulph of Mexico, from the Atlantic to the Pacific, revenue is to be collected and expended, armies are to be marched and supported. The exigencies of the nation may require that the treasure raised in the north should be transported to the south, *that* raised in the east conveyed to the west, or that this order should be reversed. Is that construction of the constitution to be preferred which would render these operations difficult, hazardous, and expensive? Can we adopt that construction, (unless the words imperiously require it), which would impute to the framers of that instruments, when granting these powers for the public good, the intention of impeding their exercise by withholding a choice of means? If, indeed, such be the mandate of the constitution, we have only to obey; but that instrument does not profess to enumerate the means by which the powers it confers may be executed; nor does it prohibit the creation of a corporation, if the existence of such a being be essential to the beneficial exercise of those powers. It is, then, the subject of fair inquiry, how far such means may be employed. (*McCulloch*, 406–9)

These two paragraphs have influenced many of those who have thought about our constitution. What are the secrets of this power? Many of those who have been influenced have carried away from their reading the "theory" Marshall propounds. But they have not often noticed the "story" Marshall tells, nor have they been alert to the links between the story and the theory. John Marshall does have a "theory" about interpreting the Constitution. He asserts that it is not "a legal code," and thus it is not be read in the way he read it in *Marbury*. A narrow and technical passing of language is inappropriate; for example, we should not expect to find in the text "accurate detail." According to Marshall, we cannot read this document correctly unless we understand that it differs from the ordinary legal instrument. "Its nature . . . requires, that only its great outlines should be marked, its important objects designated, and the minor ingredients which compose those objects be deduced from the nature of the objects themselves." As Charles Black so aptly puts it, one does not deduce directly from the text, but from the structure that the text establishes. [9] Marshall summarizes his thesis—we can't interpret a document unless we understand what kind of document we are reading—in his justly famous delphic utterance: "We must never forget, that it is *a constitution* we are expounding." Marshall states his theory elegantly. I can testify (based on personal observation) that his words have had a powerful impact on those of us who teach constitutional law. I do not wish to add to the commentary that builds on Marshall. [10] Instead, I wish to highlight those moments of explicit and implicit narrative in Marshall's account.

Marshall weaves his narrative into his theory so subtly that one can miss it. We can discern Marshall's art by reviewing the first paragraph of the two I have quoted. This paragraph starts with a simple observation—the power of incorporating a bank is not explicitly listed as one of Congress's enumerated powers. However, Marshall then points out that the Constitution does not contain the clause present in the Articles of Confederation that expressly "excludes incidental or implied powers." [11] By itself, the mere act of contrasting the documents of 1777 and 1787 does not constitute narrative, but it hints at one. Marshall is asserting that the difference in language is important, which entails (in this context) that the two documents are historically linked, which further entails some sort of historical narrative to explain the link.

Marshall extends this collocation of documents by quoting the actual language of the Tenth Amendment, which was drafted in 1789. The quotation is prefaced by the following: "Even the 10th amendment, which was framed for the purpose of quieting the excessive jealousies which had been excited, omits the word 'expressly.'" In this passage, the narrative begins to surface, although the actors have not yet been named. Marshall states that the language "was framed" for a particular "purpose," which entails human agency. The narrative becomes explicit in the next sentence: "The men who

9. Charles L. Black, *Structure and Relation in Constitutional Law* (Baton Rouge: Louisiana State University Press, 1969).

10. Black's *Structure and Relation in Constitutional Law* is a "classic." And more recently, Philip Bobbitt, *Constitutional Interpretation* (Cambridge, Mass.: Basil Blackwell, 1991), has extended this genre of commentary in a new direction.

11. *McCulloch*, 406. Marshall is alluding to Article II of the Articles of Confederation, which reads: "Each State retains its sovereignty, freedom and independence, and every power, jurisdiction and right, which is not by this confederation expressly delegated to the United States, in Congress Assembled."

drew and adopted this amendment had experienced the embarrassments resulting from the insertion of this word [expressly] in the articles of confederation, and probably omitted it to avoid these embarrassments." We now have the narrative made explicit. According to Marshall's story, both those who drafted the amendment and those who voted to accept it shared a common purpose, and their acts—choosing words, enacting words into law—were performed to carry out their common purpose.

This story, to be sure, is fiction, but attributing purpose is also one of our most common legal fictions, perhaps beneficent, almost surely necessary. Marshall has done what lawyers quite commonly do; he has asked, "Why did they say that? And furthermore, why that particular choice of words?" This question about "the why" of a document is always relevant and appropriate. Legal documents (be they humble like contracts or elevated like constitutions) are practical documents; they are supposed to do something. Consequently, it is always relevant and appropriate to ask what the drafters were trying to do. Unfortunately, good questions do not always have good answers. Although we should ask what those who drafted and voted were trying to do, it does not follow that we will be able to get a good answer. First, those who acted were a diverse group; they had disagreements. They may have compromised their disagreements into a final text, but if so, each probably had different reasons for believing that the compromise was acceptable. In short, although each had a purpose, it does not follow that there was a common purpose. Second, hindsight is better than foresight, and we must be cautious lest we attribute a clarity of purpose to the actors that they did not in fact have. Looking back, we can imagine that the drafters saw the significance of omitting or including the word "expressly." But at the time they may have had only dim expectations about the consequences of their words; even if they intended to be making a change, they may have had only a vague idea about what the change would be. And finally, when we say that the details of the document (word choice, sentence structure, omitted words, and so forth) reveal the drafter's purpose, we may be overlooking the possibility that the detail that strikes us may have been the product of carelessness, thoughtlessness, or simple accident. In short, we always need to ask what they were trying to do with those words in this document, but we may not be able to get good answers.

John Marshall did not consider these possibilities, but if he had, he still might have written the same opinion. These caveats are merely doubts; they are not refutations. It could well be that a careful investigation would remove all doubts and prove that Marshall was right. Perhaps. My own belief is that such doubts cannot be removed or sustained. They cannot be removed, because even historical "proof" cannot eliminate all plausible doubt, and they cannot be sustained because the record is incomplete. However, these doubts about Marshall's story are not fatal, since his story does not stand alone in this opinion; his story gains strength from the way it goes together with his theory.

Marshall's story—those who drafted the Constitution omitted the word "expressly" so as to avoid "the embarrassments" that our government experienced under the Articles of Confederation—is woven together with his theory about the nature of the Constitution. Indeed, he shifts back and forth between these two modes of thought. For example, he follows the sentence which asserts that those "who drew and adopted this [the tenth] amendment" had "probably omitted it [the word 'expressly'] to avoid those embarrassments" with the abstract and theorizing sentence in which he asserts that any constitution which accurately specified all of the relevant details "would partake of the prolixity of a legal code, and could scarcely be embraced by the human mind." Indeed, such prolixity would be a vice: "[Such a constitution] would probably never be understood by the public." And since Marshall's political theory derives all power from the people, it follows that a constitution which could not "be understood by the public" would not be a constitution, only an attempt at one.

If it is true that a constitution must "be understood by the public" in order to be a constitution, then the conclusion is obvious: "Its nature, therefore, requires, that only its great outlines should be marked." I think that no one can read these marvelous sentences without being impressed by the power of Marshall's mind, and I also think that one of the secrets of his power is his skill in weaving together story and theory. This power is displayed in his prose, which now returns to his narrative. Having asserted on theoretical grounds that a constitution should be concise and general, Marshall resumes his story about the drafters to corroborate his conclusion. "That this idea was entertained by the framers of the American constitution, is not only to be inferred from the nature of the instrument, but from the language." In other words, since the framers wrote a short document, we can infer that they thought conciseness was desirable, from which we can infer that they held Marshall's theory about why conciseness is desirable. In these passages, Marshall weaves story and theory together in a way that strengthens both. His theory about the "nature" of the Constitution gains authority by the story that this theory is not his alone, but also held by the drafters. And conversely, his story about the drafters is made stronger and more plausible by his theory, which explains that the drafters wrote such a short document because they knew what they were doing and that they did their job well.

At this point in the opinion, Marshall sums up this double argument that the drafters intended what theory demands—a document in which only the "great outlines" are inscribed—by his famous delphic utterance: "In considering this question [of how to read the Constitution], then, we must never forget, that it is *a constitution* we are expounding." I have used the world "delphic" to characterize this sentence since it strikes the average reader as both profound and obscure. This sentence stands to our scholarship in constitutional law just as the words of the Delphic Oracle stand to the philosophy of Socrates. We scholars accept the authority of our oracle, and then we try to figure out what it means. (However, Socrates was more serious about his quest than we are about ours.) My own guess is that the obscure difficulties of this sentence can be traced to its double role in both theory and story: it sums up a story; it restates a theory. Constitution making was a relatively new practice at the end of the eighteenth century, and when Marshall wrote this opinion, he was only three decades removed from the effective date of the instrument that we call our constitution. This document was the product of a political struggle, but there was also an intellectual struggle. Which words should be chosen? How should they be arranged? Their achievement was extraordinary, perhaps unique. The story can be told in many ways. If I understand Marshall correctly, he wants to remind us that we can lose what was gained if we fail to understand the how and why of the drafting. The urgent tone of his words "we must never forget" bear witness to Marshall's fear that we will forget what the framers knew about drafting a constitution and that forgetting would be a disaster.

This great sentence, with its appeal to us to remember belongs to a story-teller. To value memory is to honor the past. But Marshall also speaks as a theorist, since what he wants us to remember is a proposition; he wants us to remember "that it is *a constitution* we are expounding." The theoretical generality of Marshall's claim is emphasized by his use of the indefinite article. He had used the indefinite article once before in this very paragraph; he asserted that "a constitution," were it to contain all of the details, would be too prolix. And now, here at the end of the paragraph, he repeats the phrase and this time puts it in italics. Marshall may adhere to the Platonic thesis that one cannot properly construe *the constitution* (the historically specific document) except in light of *a constitution* (an ideal type). Or perhaps his thesis is more modest; he may be restating his thesis that a *constitution* is not a *statute*. The earlier parts of the paragraph authorize either interpretation: he has tried to elucidate the task of reading the Constitution by contrasting a constitution with a statute; he has also emphasized the "nature" of a constitution. Indeed, perhaps we must apply all of those distinctions to Marshall's oracular utterance if we are to understand it.[12]

If I am right that Marshall's prose sweeps forward so powerfully because of the skill with which he weaves together narrative and theory, then perhaps it is also true that his prose would not persuade if he had relied on only one mode of discourse. I have already noted how his narrative is vulnerable to attack. Marshall's story about the drafting process is reductively simplistic. He supposes a clarity of purpose where vagueness is more probable; he postulates a unity of purpose where conflict was surely present. Marshall's theory is equally vulnerable. The assertion that a lengthy and detailed document would fail politically, that a prolix constitution would miscarry, is also dubious. After all, our brief, but comprehensive constitution, its "great outlines" notwithstanding, is generally unread. Be honest: who among you have ever read the document in question straight through to the end? And even if you have, do you know anyone else who has? On the other hand, consider such documents as the Torah, the Gospels, or the Koran. (I list them in chronological order.) These documents are the "constitutions" of certain religious communities, and they are far more complex—and much, much longer—than our political constitution. One might ponder the irony that very few law professors (who generally imagine themselves to be sophisticated intellectuals) have sat down with the Constitution and seriously contemplated its mysteries, whereas quite ordinary members of religious communities are serious about reading their text. Leviticus is far more daunting than the United States Constitution, and yet more of our fellow citizens have read it. Law students and their professors in fact don't really study the Constitution; they study John Marshall's opinions.

This discrepancy—religious communicants have read their constitutions, but the legal community has not read its—can be explained if we acknowledge that stories are necessary. The Torah, the Gospels, and the Koran are rich in aphorisms, injunctions, narrative, philosophy, and parables; and

---

12. In Samuel Johnson's *Dictionary of the English Language* (1755) the legal references of "constitution" are sixth and seventh in a series of seven definitions. The first definition uses the word as a verbal. Definitions 2 through 5 refer to natural qualities. To illustrate constitution as "temper of body," Johnson quotes John Dryden's statement. "Beauty is nothing else but a just accord and mutual harmony of the members, animated by a healthful *constitution.*" Johnson quotes Shakespeare's *Merchant of Venice* for constitution as "temper of mind": "Some dear friend dead, else nothing else in the world" / Could turn so much the *constitution* / Of any constant man."

each type of discourse, such as the aphorism, is made more powerful by being juxtaposed to other ways of speaking. By this standard, the United States Constitution is impoverished. And so it is no surprise that something more is needed to make it come alive. John Marshall had the genius to give us that something more; he showed us how to combine story and theory and thus re-create the Constitution. As a result, lawyers read Marshall, not the original. His voice is so powerful that it has replaced the voice of the original.[13]

If we grant Marshall's proposition that the details are to be deduced from the "great outlines," how should the deducing be done? The second of the two paragraphs that I have quoted shows us how Marshall does it. Marshall's performance is splendid, and its splendor comes from his mastery of different modes of discourse. He doesn't voice the single line of a melody; his voice generates the multiple lines of a chorus. Marshall begins with an abstract description of the "great outlines" of the powers granted to the national government, and the vocabulary of this abstract description is largely derived from the language of the Constitution itself:

> Although, among the enumerated powers of government, we do not find the word "bank" or "incorporation," we find the great powers to lay and collect taxes; to borrow money; to regulate commerce; to declare and conduct a war; to raise and support armies and navies.

But Marshall does not rest here; he restates his abstract argument with concrete metaphors:

> The sword and the purse, all the external relations, and no inconsiderable portion of the industry of the nation, are entrusted to its government.

Having described the "great outlines" in two different modes, Marshall switches to the dialectic of argument:

> It can never be pretended that these vast powers draw after them others of inferior importance, merely because they are inferior. Such

13. See James Boyd White, *When Words Lose Their Meaning: Constitutions and Reconstitutions of Language, Character, and Community* (Chicago: University of Chicago Press, 1984), 263: "Marshall's opinion seems to be less an interpretation of the Constitution than an amendment to it, . . . [it seems] continuous with the original text."

an idea can never be advanced. But it may with great reason be contended, that a government, entrusted with such ample powers, on the due execution of which the happiness and prosperity of the nation so vitally depends, must also be entrusted with ample means for their execution.

Arguments have conclusions, so Marshall next adopts the voice of sweeping generalization to assert his conclusion:

The power being given, it is the interest of the nation to facilitate its execution. It can never be their interest, and cannot be presumed to have been their intention, to clog and embarrass its execution by withholding the most appropriate means.

The rationale of this conclusion is built on the concepts of "interest" and "intention" and thus partially replicates the interplay between theory and story of the previous paragraph. But the conclusion is not left to rest on deduction. Marshall next turns to the practical consequences of constitutional interpretation.

As a prelude to considering the practical consequences, one must have some way of describing them. In order to do so, Marshall switches voice once again. In the passage quoted above, he described the Constitution using both a language drawn from the text and metaphors ("sword," "purse," "industry") external to it. The metaphors are perhaps more vivid than the textual vocabulary, but only marginally so; the language of the text is itself rather straightforward. However, these descriptions, even though they are strikingly economical, are also rather static. But as Marshall sets the stage for his argument from practical consequences, his description becomes dynamic. He pictures a world in motion:

Throughout this vast republic, from the St. Croix to the Gulph of Mexico, from the Atlantic to the Pacific, revenue is to be collected and expended, armies are to be marched and supported. The exigencies of the nation may require that the treasure raised in the north should be transported to the south, *that* raised in the east conveyed to the west, or that this order should be reversed.

To be sure, there is what one might call a "technical inaccuracy" in Marshall's description; were I describing the geographic bounds of the Republic circa 1819, I would not put the borders exactly where Marshall put them, but let us pass by such details and attend to the rhetoric; after all, one could say that the inaccuracy merely shows that Marshall was ahead of his time.

The rhetoric of these two sentences quickens the paragraph. One is pulled out of the books and into the world. The arena of action in this world is vast; it is a continent. Armies and revenue must be moved from one end of the continent to the other. And the implication is surely that vast motion entails vast power. Consequently, it is natural for the next move in the paragraph to be a rhetorical question. If geography is the argument, one needs nothing more than a rhetorical question.

> Is that construction of the constitution to be preferred which would render these operations difficult, hazardous, and expensive? Can we adopt that construction, (unless the words imperiously require it,) which would impute to the framers of that instrument, when granting these powers for the public good, the intention of impeding their exercise by withholding a choice of means?

Surely *not*, I answer, and who could say otherwise? The game is up; Marshall has won. To be sure, this victory must be consolidated by attending to some details, and so part 1 of the opinion (Congressional power) contains another sixteen pages. But if you haven't been persuaded by now, there is nothing between here and the end of the opinion that will change your mind.

III

There is, however, one more passage in the opinion that is worth considering, and it is important since it displays Marshall's vision of the Constitution. The occasion for this visionary utterance is the interpretation of those words in the document that lawyers call "the necessary and proper clause." The clause appears in Article I, Section 8, wherein congressional power is delineated. Section 8 begins by stating, "The Congress shall have Power . . . ," and then proceeds to explain with eighteen infinitives what Congress "shall have Power" to do, such as "To borrow Money on the credit of the United States." The eighteenth and last is "To make all Laws which shall be necessary and proper for carrying into Execution the foregoing Powers, and all other Powers vested in this Constitution in the Government of the United States, or in any Department or Officer thereof."

Counsel for Maryland argued that a bank was not "necessary" to execute any of "the foregoing Powers," and thus the Congress did not have power to issue a corporate charter to such a bank. This argument wins the day if "necessary" means "indispensable." But as Marshall quite properly notes, the word "necessary," like any other word, has a range of possible meanings. This being so, one must construe and interpret the word by considering "the subject, the context, the intention of the person using [the word]" (*McCulloch*, 415). Marshall proceeds to elaborate "the subject, the context, the intention," and in doing so, he also elaborates his vision of "*a constitution.*"

> Let this be done in the case under consideration. The subject is the execution of those great powers on which the welfare of a nation essentially depends. It must have been the intention of those who gave these powers, to insure, as far as human prudence could insure, their beneficial execution. This could not be done by confiding the choice of means to such narrow limits as not to leave it in the power of Congress to adopt any which might be appropriate, and which were conducive to the end. This provision is made in a constitution intended to endure for ages to come, and, consequently, to be adapted to the various *crises* of human affairs. To have prescribed the means by which government should, in all future time, execute its powers, would have been to change, entirely, the character of the instrument, and give it the properties of a legal code. It would have been an unwise attempt to provide, by immutable rules, for exigencies which, if foreseen at all, must have been seen dimly, and which can be best provided for as they occur. To have declared that the best means shall not be used, but those alone without which the power given would be nugatory, would have been to deprive the legislature of the capacity to avail itself of experience, to exercise its reason, and to accommodate its legislation to circumstances. If we apply this principle of construction to any of the powers of the government, we shall find it so pernicious in its operation that we shall be compelled to discard it. (415–16)

The theme of this paragraph is change and growth: there will be change in the world; the government must grow in order to respond to change; the

Constitution must be interpreted to make response to change possible, for the "constitution [is] intended to endure for ages to come, and, consequently, to be adapted to the various *crises* of human affairs." In the world of change, "immutable rules" (the sort of rules which *Marbury* declared necessary!) would be foolish, indeed dangerous. If we impose rules on the legislature, then we will "deprive the legislature of the capacity to avail itself of experience, to exercise its reason, and to accommodate its legislation to circumstances," and the rhetorical flourish of this passage declares that these consequences would be disastrous. In *Marbury*, the claim was that the rules must be enforced, or else the Constitution would be meaningless; it could be altered by an ordinary legislative act. In *McCulloch*, the rules themselves are a threat to the Constitution, since if we enforce them "we shall find it so pernicious in its operation that we shall be compelled to discard it."

   This story of change and growth has been echoed by some of Marshall's greatest successors. For example, in *Missouri v. Holland*,[14] the justices had to construe the several clauses in the Constitution that are relevant to the national power to make treaties. The treaty at issue was a forerunner of what is today called an "environmental" or "ecological" issue; the treaty was adopted to protect migratory birds from excessive hunting. We as a people are today quite comfortable with the idea that the national government has the power to make treaties to protect the environment, and to enact statutes in support of such treaties. But in 1920, the date of the case, there was no consensus. The regulation and management of wild game animals was traditionally the province of state government, and there was no consensus (indeed, it was highly controversial) that the national government could take over this state prerogative by making a treaty. Could the treaty power be used for such novel purposes? Justice Holmes wrote the following:

   When we are dealing with words that also are a constituent act, like the Constitution of the United States, we must realize that they [the words] have called into life a being the development of which could not have been foreseen completely by the most gifted of its begetters. It was enough for them to realize or to hope that they had created an organism; it has taken a century and has cost their successors much sweat and blood to prove that they created a nation. The case before us must be considered in the light of our whole experience and

14. 252 U.S. 416 (1920).

not merely in that of what was said a hundred years ago. (*Missouri v. Holland*, 433)

It should come as no surprise that Holmes and his colleagues held that the treaty was valid.

In 1954, the Supreme Court decided in *Brown v. Board of Education* that a state legislature could not establish schools in which children were segregated by race.[15] Like Holmes, Chief Justice Earl Warren echoed Marshall on growth and change, and like Holmes, he did so without explicitly citing him. Warren had more of a pressing need to appeal to change than Holmes did, since the Supreme Court had asked counsel to argue the historical issue: "What evidence is there that the Congress which submitted and the state legislatures and conventions which ratified the Fourteenth Amendment contemplated or did not contemplate, understood or did not understand, that it would abolish segregation in public schools?"[16]

Alas, the answer to the question depends on how one interprets it. One might interpret the question by asking, Was school segregation on the list of "evils" which they hoped would be speedily eliminated? So interpreted, the answer is obviously no. However, if one asks, Did they intend to limit the application of the Fourteenth Amendment to a finite and particular set of evils, those which they identified? Then the answer would once again be no. Of course, we might try to probe more deeply into the psychology of the drafters and notifiers and ask, Would they generally approve of segregated schools? Probably yes. But then, why should such psychological speculation be relevant? Those who voted in favor of the Fourteenth Amendment differed among themselves—some believed in establishing full racial equality before the law, whereas others would restrict racial equality to a limited set of fundamental rights—and so they hid their disagreements by adopting vague and general language. Warren cut through this sort of controversy by declaring the question asked to be irrelevant. He quite properly noted that public education was not then universally recognized as a responsibility of government. Free public schools were rare in the South, and even in the

15. 347 U.S. 483 (1954).

16. *Brown v. Board of Education*, 345 U.S. 972 (1953). The court was split after argument, and so to buy time, the judges ordered reargument and asked the parties to address five questions; the question quoted was the first. For an account, see Richard Kluger, *Simple Justice: The History of Brown v. Board of Education and Black America's Struggle for Equality* (New York: Alfred A. Knopf, 1975), and Mark Tushnet, "What Really Happened in Brown v. Board of Education," 91 *Colum. L. Rev.* 1867 (1991).

North, their establishment was recent and their development rudimentary.[17]
In other words, Warren concluded that conditions then were different from
conditions now, and thus, interpretation must reflect this change. He stated:
"In approaching this problem, we cannot turn the clock back to 1868 when
the Amendment was adopted. . . . We must consider public education in
the light of its full development and its present place in American life
throughout the Nation. Only in this way can it be determined if segregation
in public schools deprives these plaintiffs of the equal protection of the
laws."[18]

I cite the quotations from Holmes and Warren merely as illustrations,
not proof. I do not wish to prove a historical thesis about whether Holmes
or Warren derived their notion of a "living constitution"[19] from John Marshall or from some other source. Instead, I wish merely to illustrate how
"growth" can be invoked by one who is called upon to interpret the
Constitution.

These two stories—that of static limits in *Marbury*, and that of dynamic
growth in *McCulloch*—are complicated. On the one hand, they are stories
that can be told from outside the law. For example, historians of legal
practice might use these stories of the static and the dynamic to elucidate
their data, to shape their evidence into a form that one could understand.
On the other hand, Marshall's successors can use these stories in their work
within the legal system. When judges interpret the Constitution, they can
go about their job as though they should be pinning down limits, or alternatively, as though they should be furthering the dynamics of growth. Moreover, both historians and judges can emulate Marshall by shifting back
and forth un(self-)consciously, speaking different ways on different topics.
Unfortunately, the vexed topic of equality is one of those topics we want
both ways at once, limited and growing, which makes the stories about
equality rich with complexity.

17. *Brown v. Board of Education*, 347 U.S. 489–90.
18. Ibid., 492–93.
19. The phrase, "a living constitution," is commonly used in the press.

4

The Story of Equality

I cannot prove that the stories of *Marbury* and *McCulloch* are *the* fundamental stories of constitutional law. My judgment is nothing more than a subjective impression based on my experience of having taught constitutional law for several decades; but I take some comfort in knowing that it is not idiosyncratic. Duncan Kennedy asserts that analogous polarities run through the entire structure of private law.[1] and John Leubsdorf asserts that a careful reading of the Constitution reveals that the polarity of *Marbury* and *McCulloch* can be found in the constitutional text itself.[2] However, I did not write Chapters 2 and 3 for the undeniable pleasure of corroborating what others have said. I wrote them in an attempt to reduce the confusion over the

1. Duncan Kennedy, "Form and Substance in Private Law Adjudication," 89 *Harv. L. Rev.* 1685 (1976).
2. John Leubsdorf, "Deconstructing the Constitution," 40 *Stanford L. Rev.* 181 (1987).

topic of racial equality that has been aggravated by the disorienting way that we switch back and forth between two different stories. Since I also think that we must solve the general problems of equality and the particular problems of racial equality if we are to live up to the name of democracy, I am confident that thinking carefully about these two stories may (but need not) contribute to the health of our polity.

I

Equality has been one of the ideals proclaimed in American history. Ever since de Tocqueville drew the sharp distinction between Europe and the United States with regard to equality, it has been marked as one of the distinguishing characteristics of our culture. It did not start out that way. In the colonial era, the culture, economics, and politics of the Colonies (of those who were the *subjects* of the Crown) were distinctly nonegalitarian. To be sure, there was a strong spirit of liberty; but a sense of liberty is not inconsistent with hierarchy. Those who live in a hierarchy can be zealous in protecting their place in it, and they can be prickly in asserting their customary rights. It all depends on the circumstances, and in the right circumstances, the sense of "rights" in a hierarchy can develop into a keen sense of liberty. In the American colonies, and in England, hierarchy combined with liberty. The American Revolution decisively changed the hierarchical structure that preexisted it. After the Revolution, authority could no longer be derived from the authority of the Crown. A new sovereign was declared—The People.[3] The consequences of this change were unknown when it was made, and perhaps it can be said that they are not yet fully known even today. One of the unknowns has been the scope of the principle of equality. We have witnessed claims to equality in race, gender, national origin, religion, and economic status. There have been sharp disagreements about whether the claims should be honored, and if so, what honoring them would entail. (By the way, one should note that my list of claims is not authoritative; items come and go. For example, the claim to economic equality has fallen on hard times lately, whereas new items, such as equality for different sexual preferences, seem to be gaining ground.)

3. See, generally, Gordon S. Wood, *The Radicalism of the American Revolution* (New York: Knopf, 1992), and Edmund S. Morgan, *Inventing the People* (New York: Norton, 1988).

The story of equality, however it should be told, did not get its start with the document that we call the Constitution. The Constitution of 1787 never mentions the word; however, it does not mention slavery either. Indeed, it uses elaborate euphemisms to avoid admitting the existence of the institution of slavery. This document, unlike the Declaration of Independence, equivocates, endorsing neither equality nor inequality. In the famous *Dred Scott* case, Chief Justice Taney attempted to remove the equivocations and contradictions by stating that the Constitution endorsed slavery and that the Declaration of Independence was irrelevant. In his opinion, Taney quoted the famous words of the Declaration:

> We hold these truths to be self-evident: that all men are created equal; that they are endowed by their Creator with certain unalienable rights; that among them is life, liberty, and the pursuit of happiness; that to secure these rights, Governments are instituted, deriving their just powers from the consent of the government.[4]

Taney proceeded to declare the irrelevance of these words in the following:

> The general words above quoted would seem to embrace the whole human family, and if they were used in a similar instrument at this day would be so understood. But it is too clear for dispute, that the enslaved African race were not intended to be included, and formed no part of the people who framed and adopted this declaration; for if the language, as understood in that day, would embrace them, the conduct of the distinguished men who framed the Declaration of Independence would have been utterly and flagrantly inconsistent with the principles they asserted; and instead of the sympathy of mankind, to which they so confidently appealed, they would have deserved and received universal rebuke and reprobation.
>
> Yet the men who framed this declaration were great men—high in literary acquirement—high in their sense of honor, and incapable of asserting principles inconsistent with those on which they were acting. They perfectly understood the meaning of the language they used, and how it would be understood by others; and they knew that it would not in any part of the civilized world be supposed to embrace the negro race, which, by common consent, had been excluded from

4. *Dred Scott v. Sanford*, 19 How. 393, 410 (1857).

civilized Governments and the family of nations, and doomed to slavery. They spoke and acted according to the then established doctrines and principles, and in the ordinary language of the day, and no one misunderstood them. (*Dred Scott*, 410)

In a speech that was a prelude to the famous Lincoln-Douglas debate, Stephen Douglas endorsed Taney's interpretation of the Declaration of Independence as follows:

> No man can vindicate the character, motives and conduct of the signers of the Declaration of Independence, except upon the hypothesis that they referred to the white race alone, and not to the African, when they declared all men to have been created equal— that they were speaking of British subjects on this continent being equal to British subjects born and residing in Great Britain—that they were entitled to the same inalienable rights, and among them were enumerated life, liberty and the pursuit of happiness. The Declaration was adopted for the purpose of justifying the colonists in the eyes of the civilized world in withdrawing their allegiance from the British crown, and dissolving their connection with the mother country.[5]

There are many things wrong with Taney's and Douglas's interpretation of the Declaration of Independence. For one thing, they assume a perfect consistency between word and action (and a consistency judged by the standards of posterity) that has never existed in the history of humanity. In all of human affairs, inconsistency is the rule, consistency the exception. Furthermore, there is a historical mistake, in that the members of the Revolutionary era were quite well aware of their inconsistency and knew full well that their words did not match their deeds. Let me cite a single example: Thomas Jefferson himself, in the only book he published, *Notes on the State of Virginia* (1787), was explicit on the evils of slavery, asserted that it was inconsistent with the principles on which our liberties were founded, and stated, "Indeed, I tremble for my country when I reflect that God is just."[6] But their error is deeper perhaps than their simplistic psychology and

---

5. Abraham Lincoln, *Speeches and Writings, 1832–1858*, ed. Don E. Fehrenbacher (New York: Library of America, 1989), 399.
6. Thomas Jefferson, *Notes on the State of Virginia*, ed. William Peden (New York: Norton, 1972), 162–63.

history. Victor Rosenblum once said to me in conversation that their error was at bottom theological, in that Douglas and Taney ruled out the possibility that public language might be a vow, that one might promise to do better than one has done.

Abraham Lincoln's response was sharp. To Stephen Douglas he responded with ridicule:

> My good friends, read that carefully over some leisure hour, and ponder well upon it—see what a mere wreck—mangled ruin—it makes of our once glorious Declaration.
>
> "They were speaking of British subjects on this continent being equal to British subjects born and residing in Great Britain!" Why, according to this, not only negroes but white people outside of Great Britain and America are not spoken of in that instrument. The English, Irish and Scotch, along with white Americans, were included, to be sure, but the French, Germans, and other white people of the world are all gone to the pot along with the Judge's [Lincoln referred to Douglas as judge] inferior races.
>
> I had thought the Declaration promised something better than the condition of British subjects; but no, it only meant that we should be *equal* to them in their own oppressed and *unequal* condition. According to that, it gave no promise that, having kicked off the King and Lords of Great Britain, we should not at once be saddled with a King and Lords of our own.
>
> I had thought the Declaration contemplated the progressive improvement in the condition of all men everywhere; but no, it merely "was adopted for the purpose of justifying the colonists in the eyes of the civilized world in withdrawing their allegiance from the British crown, and dissolving their connection with the mother country." Why, that object having been effected some eighty years ago, the Declaration is of no practical use now—mere rubbish—old wadding left to rot on the battle-field after the victory is won.
>
> I understand you are preparing to celebrate the "Fourth" tomorrow week. What for? The doings of that day had no reference to the present; and quite half of you are not even descendants of those who were referred to at that day. But I suppose you will celebrate; and will even go so far as to read the Declaration. Suppose after you read it once in the old-fashioned way, you read it once more with Judge Douglas's version. It will then run thus: "We hold these truths to be

self-evident that all British subjects who were on this continent eighty-one years ago, were created equal to all British subjects born and *then* residing in Great Britain."

And now I appeal to all—to Democrats as well as others—are you really willing that the Declaration shall be thus frittered away?—thus left no more at most, than an interesting memorial of the dead past? thus shorn of its vitality, and practical value; and left without the *germ* or even the *suggestion* of the individual rights of man in it?[7]

Lincoln's response to Taney's opinion was equally sharp:

Chief Justice Taney, in his opinion in the Dred Scott case, admits that the language of the Declaration is broad enough to include the whole human family, but he and Judge Douglas argue that the authors of that instrument did not intend to include negroes, by the fact that they did not at once, actually place them on an equality with the whites. Now this grave argument comes to just nothing at all, by the other fact, that they did not at once, *or ever afterwards*, actually place all white people on an equality with one or another. And this is the staple argument of both the Chief Justice and the Senator, for doing this obvious violence to the plain, unmistakable language of the Declaration.

I think the authors of that notable instrument intended to include *all* men, but they did not intend to declare all men equal *in all respects*. They did not mean to say all were equal in color, size, intellect, moral developments, or social capacity. They defined with tolerable distinctness, in what respects they did consider all men created equal—equal in "certain inalienable rights, among which are life, liberty, and the pursuit of happiness."

This they said, and this meant. They did not mean to assert the obvious untruth, that all were then actually enjoying that equality, nor yet, that they were about to confer it immediately upon them. In fact they had no power to confer such a boon. They meant simply to declare the *right*, so that the *enforcement* of it might follow as fast as circumstances should permit.

They meant to set up a standard maxim for free society, which should be familiar to all, and revered by all; constantly looked to,

7. Lincoln, *Speeches and Writings*, 399–400.

constantly labored for, and even though never perfectly attained, constantly approximated, and thereby constantly spreading and deepening its influence, and augmenting the happiness and value of life to all people of all colors everywhere. The assertion that "all men are created equal" was of no practical use in effecting our separation from Great Britain; and it was placed in the Declaration, not for that, but for future use. Its authors meant it to be, thank God, it is now proving itself, a stumbling block to those who in after times might seek to turn a free people back into the hateful paths of despotism. They knew the proneness of prosperity to breed tyrants, and they meant when such should re-appear in this fair land and commence their vocation they should find left for them at least one hard nut to crack.[8]

Mortimer J. Adler and William Gorman put Lincoln's position rather nicely in the following two paragraphs:

A term from the Greek political lexicon can help to convey what Lincoln was at some pains to say. In Aristotle's political philosophy, the *politeia* is what gives a particular *polis*—a particular city or state—its distinctive character. There is no single English word that will serve as a translation of "*politeia*," but its meaning can be expressed by speaking of the formative principles that shape a political community. By analogy with the relation of soul to body in living organisms, Aristotle thought of the *politeia* as the soul of the body politic, because it is the animating principle that gives form and purpose to a political community. The *politeia* is, therefore, antecedent to and deeper than the constitution. The constitution, which consists in a definition and arrangement of offices, is devised to accord with and to serve the *politeia*. Substantive legislation under the constitution represents an effort to direct the political life in conformity with the *politeia*. In Aristotle's lexicon, a "revolution" is a change in the *politeia*. Any constitutional change or any major legislative policy in strong and durable violation of the *politeia* is a revolution.

It is clear from the words that Lincoln spoke in Independence Hall, and from his persistent invocation of the Declaration in many

8. Ibid., 398–99.

contexts, that he held the American *politeia* to have been revealed in the Declaration of Independence. The nation was born—one might say "besouled"—with the Declaration. Against Stephen Douglas, who proposed to allow each new territory to decide for itself whether it wanted the institution of slavery, and also against Chief Justice Roger B. Taney, who interpreted the Constitution as prohibiting any federal act to prevent the extension of slavery, Lincoln always appealed to the controlling authority of the Declaration, with its pivotal assertion of the equality of men. Any sophistical evasion of that proposition or any policy contravening its exigencies would be a revolutionary breach of the *politeia*.[9]

Adler and Gorman's use of the Greek word *politeia* conveys admirably what is at stake. I share their hope that the distinction is worth making, that one needs to understand the distinction between the fundamental principle of equality and the legal structure of constitutionalism that we hope might execute that principle. By understanding the distinction, one is able to ask, How far does the Constitution go in executing the principle of equality? However, even if one asks the question, there is more than one story that can be told in answering it.

II

The legal story of equality might be said to start with the Civil War amendments. The Thirteenth Amendment (1865) abolished slavery; the Fourteenth Amendment (1868) prescribed the terms by which the rebel states could rejoin the union and proclaimed a national power to protect the privileges and immunities of citizenship and to guarantee due process of law and equal protection of law; the Fifteenth Amendment (1870) declared that the right to vote should not be denied on racial grounds. (The dates that I have cited above are the dates each amendment was ratified.) However, the dates cited above, 1865–70, mark the formal date, not the effective date, of the legal story about equality. The judges gutted the amendments. The

---

9. Mortimer J. Adler and William Gorman, "Reflections: The Gettysburg Address," *New Yorker*, 8 September 1975, 42–43. For an analogous description of Lincoln's political thought, see Garry Wills, *Lincoln at Gettysburg* (New York: Simon & Schuster, 1992).

first blow fell in the *Slaughterhouse* case,[10] in which the privileges and immunities clause of the Fourteenth was "interpreted" into uselessness and irrelevance. The *Slaughterhouse* interpretation was as clever as it was malign, and in order to display the cleverness, let me start by quoting the text.

Section 1 of the Fourteenth Amendment comprises only two sentences. It reads as follows:

> All persons born or naturalized in the United States, and subject to the jurisdiction thereof, are citizens of the United States and of the State wherein they reside. No State shall make or enforce any law which shall abridge the privileges or immunities of citizens of the United States; nor shall any State deprive any person of life, liberty, or property, without due process of law; nor deny to any person within its jurisdiction the equal protection of the laws.

The first sentence extends citizenship to everyone "born or naturalized," and it thus permits African-Americans to be citizens. But citizens of what? The text seems clear enough, but Justice Miller in *Slaughterhouse* found a subtlety in the text others might not have found. He discerned a prerequisite to state citizenship that national citizenship lacked. One becomes a citizen of this nation, of these United States, by being born within its "jurisdiction," or by being naturalized under its laws. But in order to become a citizen of a state such as New York or Louisiana, one must do more than merely be born, one must "reside" therein. Having discerned these distinct prerequisites, Miller then embraced the non sequitur that the two categories of citizenship must be distinct (*Slaughterhouse*, 73–74). Of course, one might believe that the subtlety is Miller's imposition, not drafters' intent. The drafters probably meant to do nothing more than take care of the typical case. After all, one must reside somewhere, and so the drafters declare that where one resides, there one is a citizen. In other words, the textual reference to residence is not a prerequisite; it is an allocation. Subtle problems— What about the United States citizen who has multiple residences in more than one of the several states? What about the citizen who resides overseas?—were ignored, or overlooked, or perhaps just left for another day.

Furthermore, Miller's theory of dual citizenship is not merely an imposition on the text of the Fourteenth Amendment, it is also a bad response to the historical context. Miller acknowledges that the first sentence was meant

10. 16 Wall. 36 (1873).

to overrule *Dred Scott* (73), yet the central pillar of Taney's opinion was a theory of dual citizenship. Taney knew that the legal structure of northern states such as Massachusetts acknowledged that African-Americans were entitled to state citizenship. Chief Justice Taney knew that he had no power to prevent the Massachusetts lawmakers from granting citizenship to all, but he was determined to limit the national consequences of such action. Justice Benjamin Curtis (of Massachusetts) argued in his dissent for a unitary view of citizenship; he argued that the lawmakers of each state could declare who was entitled to be a citizen, and furthermore, that whoever was a citizen of any one of the states was automatically a citizen of the United States.[11] For Curtis, citizenship was unitary, with national citizenship being derivative of state citizenship. The drafters of the Fourteenth Amendment wrote as though they too thought that citizenship was unitary, but they turned Curtis's argument upside down and made national citizenship primary, with state citizenship being derivative of national citizenship.

These theoretics about citizenship were not idle debate. For both Taney and Miller, the theory of dual citizenship was necessary to limit the sweep of the privileges and immunities clause. Taney had to limit Article IV, Section 2, the first sentence of which reads, "The Citizens of each State shall be entitled to all Privileges and Immunities of Citizens in the several States." The syntax of this sentence is obscure; one plausible hypothesis about this sentence is that its drafters intended to enact a more concise version of a similar clause, whose syntax was equally obscure, that had appeared in the Articles of Confederation, "The better to secure and perpetuate mutual friendship and intercourse among the people of the different states in this union, the free inhabitants of each of these states, paupers, vagabonds and fugitives from justice excepted, shall be entitled to all privileges and immunities of free citizens in the several states." There are several possibilities for the syntax of Article IV's privileges and immunities clause. The cryptic phrase at the end of the sentence, "in the several States," should probably be understood as though the sentence read, "Citizens . . . shall be entitled . . . [when they are] in the several States." And perhaps it would be even better to construe "in" as "throughout." Thus: "Citizens . . . shall be entitled . . . [throughout] the several States." Consider next the word "several." In the eighteenth century the "United States" were the group of states acting collectively as a nation, the "respective States" were the individual states considered separately, and the "several States" were the states

11. See *Dred Scott*, 577–79, 588.

considered as a group.[12] Consequently, we might gloss the collocation of "each" and "several" in the clause as follows: "The Citizens of each State shall be entitled . . . [throughout all] States." With this much glossing in place, there remains the hard part. When the clause refers to the "Privileges and Immunities of Citizens," which group of citizens are we talking about? Are we talking about the privileges and immunities of citizens of "the United States," or "the respective States," or "the several States"? My own judgment is that the most plausible, the least anachronistic, reading would be as follows: "The Citizens of each state shall be entitled to all Privileges and Immunities of Citizens [of the several States] in the several States."

Whatever the meaning, such a clause was potentially dangerous in the eyes of Chief Justice Taney. If free blacks were citizens of Massachusetts, and if Article IV's privileges and immunities included them, then consequences would follow which Taney found unacceptable. He stated:

> We must not confound the rights of citizenship which a State may confer within its own limits, and the rights of citizenship as a member of the Union. It does not by any means follow, because he [an African-American] has all the rights and privileges of a citizen of a State, that he must be a citizen of the United States. He may have all of the rights and privileges of the citizen of a State, and yet not be entitled to the rights and privileges of a citizen in any other State. (*Dred Scott*, 405)

The above states the conclusion. The argument for this conclusion rests on a spurious story about "intent," namely, Taney imagines that those who participated in the drafting and ratification of the document were worried then about what he is worried now, and he imagines that they must have "intended" what he would have intended were he they.

> It cannot be believed that the large slaveholding States regarded them [the African-Americans] as included in the word citizens, or would have consented to a Constitution which might compel them to receive them in that character from another state. For if they were so received, and entitled to the privileges and immunities of citizens, it would exempt them [the African-American citizens of states like

12. See Wilfred J. Ritz, *Rewriting the History of the Judiciary Act of 1789*, ed. Wythe Holt and L. H. LaRue (Norman: University of Oklahoma Press, 1990), 80–87.

Massachusetts] from the operation of the special laws and from the police regulations which they [the large shareholding states] consider to be necessary for their own safety. It would give to persons of the negro race, who were recognized as citizens in any one State of the Union, the right to enter every other State whenever they pleased, singly or in companies, without pass or passport, and without obstruction, to sojourn there as long as they pleased, to go where they pleased at every hour of the day or night without molestation, unless they committed some violation of law for which a white man would be punished; and it would give them the full liberty of speech in public and in private upon all subjects upon which its own citizens might speak; to hold public meetings upon political affairs, and to keep and carry arms wherever they went. And all of this would be done in the face of the subject race of the same color, both free and slaves, and inevitably producing discontent and insubordination among them, and endangering the peace and safety of the State. (416–17).

As Taney's flourish makes clear, the two concepts of "citizenship" and "equality" were tightly linked in antebellum America. For Taney, the sine qua non of constitutional interpretation is nonequality. The slaveholding states must be free from any duty to treat blacks and whites as equals. (And by the way, Taney was neither idiosyncratic nor eccentric in holding this position.) Taney insists that the right to free speech and the right to bear arms are rights which whites can enjoy, but not blacks. His tool for getting this result is the wedge he drives between state citizenship under state constitutions and national citizenship under the national constitution.

Miller's position in *Slaughterhouse* seems less radical. On the face of the opinion, he seems more concerned with abstractions than Taney was. He concedes that the first sentence of the Fourteenth Amendment was intended to establish the citizenship of the African-American; to that extent, equality is secured. But what is the substantive content of this new equality of citizenship? For Taney, if blacks were equal to whites in citizenship, then it followed that they would be equal in the right to speak and to bear arms. For Miller, there is to be equal citizenship, but no such consequences shall follow; or to be more precise about it, no such consequences will follow from federal law. Like Taney, Miller uses the tool of dual citizenship to limit federal power (*Slaughterhouse*, 77–78). Recall that Miller has interpreted Section 1 of the Fourteenth Amendment as recognizing the dual citizenship thesis, and since there were two types of citizenship, he concluded that there were two different sets of privileges and immunities of citizenship. And so it follows that the state will protect the state set, and the nation will protect the national set. This conclusion about which government is to protect which set of privileges and immunities is asserted explicitly in the following paragraph:

> Of the privileges and immunities of the citizen of the United States, and of the privileges and immunities of the citizen of the State, and what they respectively are, we will presently consider; but we wish to state here that it is only the former which are placed by this clause under the protection of the Federal Constitution, and that the latter, whatever they may be, are not intended to have any additional protection by this paragraph of the amendment. (74)

The dichotomy might not have been so fatal had the national list been significant, but Miller asserted that the state list contained all of the fundamental rights. Miller quoted from a pre–Civil War case in which the privileges and immunities of state citizenship were expounded in generous terms, and he endorsed the description.

> "The inquiry," he [Judge Washington] says, "is, what are the privileges and immunities of citizens of the several States? We feel no hesitation in confining these expressions to those privileges and immunities which are *fundamental*; which belong of right to the citizens of all free governments, and which have at all times been enjoyed by citizens of the several States which compose this Union, from the time of their becoming free, independent, and sovereign. What these fundamental principles, are, it would be more tedious than difficult to enumerate. They may all, however, be comprehended under the following general heads: protection by the government, with the right to acquire and possess property of every kind, and to pursue and obtain happiness and safety, subject, nevertheless, to such restraints as the government may prescribe for the general good of the whole."
>
> This definition of the privileges and immunities of citizens of the States is adopted in the main by this court in the recent case of *Ward v. The State of Maryland*, while it declines to undertake an authoritative definition beyond what was necessary to that decision.

The description, when taken to include others not named, but which are of the same general character, embraces nearly every civil right for the establishment and protection of which organized government is instituted. They are, in the language of Judge Washington, those rights which are fundamental. Throughout his opinion, they are spoken of as rights belonging to the individual as a citizen of a State. They are so spoken of in the constitutional provision which he was construing. And they have always been held to be the class of rights which the State governments were created to establish and secure. (76)

Of course, it made excellent good sense in the pre–Civil War context for the states' lists of rights to be long and the nation's short. But then, the *Slaughterhouse* case is post–Civil War, and the Constitution has been amended. In order to say that the amendments did not really change anything, Justice Miller told a story, a fictional story, about "intent." If one reads it carefully, the parallels with Taney's fictions in *Dred Scott* are striking. Miller starts by stating the status quo ante and proceeds next to flourish rhetorical questions about "intent."

It would be the vainest show of learning to attempt to prove by citations of authority, that up to the adoption of the recent amendments, no claim or pretence was set up that those [fundamental] rights depended on the Federal government for their existence or protection, beyond the very few express limitations which the Federal Constitution imposed upon the States—such, for instance, as the prohibition against ex post facto laws, bills of attainder, and laws impairing the obligation of contracts. But with the exception of these and a few other restrictions, the entire domain of the privileges and immunities of citizens of the States, as above defined, lay within the constitutional and legislative power of the States, and without that of the Federal government. Was it the purpose of the fourteenth amendment, by the simple declaration that no State should make or enforce any law which shall abridge the privileges and immunities of *citizens of the United States*, to transfer the security and protection of all the civil rights which we have mentioned, from the States to the Federal government? And where it is declared that Congress shall have the power to enforce that article, was it intended to bring within the power of Congress the entire domain of civil rights heretofore belonging exclusively to the States?

All this and more must follow, if the proposition of the plaintiffs in error be sound. For not only are these rights subject to the control of Congress whenever in its discretion any of them are supposed to be abridged by State legislation, but that body may also pass laws in advance, limiting and restricting the exercise of legislative power by the States, in their most ordinary and usual functions, as in its judgment it may think proper on all such subjects. And still further, such a construction followed by the reversal of the judgments of the Supreme Court of Louisiana in these cases, would constitute this court a perpetual censor upon all legislation of the States, on the civil rights of their own citizens, with authority to nullify such as it did not approve as consistent with those rights, as they existed at the time of the adoption of this amendment. The argument we admit is not always the most conclusive which is drawn from the consequences urged against the adoption of a particular construction of an instrument. But when, as in the case before us, these consequences are so serious, so far-reaching and pervading, so great a departure from the structure and spirit of our institutions; when the effect is to fetter and degrade the State governments by subjecting them to the control of Congress, in the exercise of powers heretofore universally conceded to them of the most ordinary and fundamental character; when in fact it radically changes the whole theory of the relations of the State and Federal governments to each other and of both these governments to the people; the argument has a force that is irresistible, in the absence of language which expresses such a purpose too clearly to admit of doubt.

We are convinced that no such results were intended by the Congress which proposed these amendments, nor by the legislatures of the States which ratified them. (77–78)

Under Miller's scheme, the national rights are limited to those which are peculiarly pertinent to the structure of national citizenship. For example, the national government has the duty and the power to protect its citizens when they exercise the privilege of filing a lawsuit in federal court, or visit a land office, or travel on the high seas, and so on (79–80). This list might strike one as rather paltry, but Miller seems to have thought it extensive enough. Of course, whether it is paltry or extensive, it is also illogical. The cases that Miller cites to generate his list of national privileges and immunities predate the Civil War, and they recognize the national government's power to protect the rights that were listed. In other words, the privileges and immunities that Miller lists were protected even before the Fourteenth Amendment's ratification. Miller's conclusion implies that the Fourteenth Amendment does not change the way privileges and immunities are protected, which seems illogical, since this construction entails that the relevant language in the Fourteenth Amendment is redundant. However, Miller is so caught up in his fiction—that the drafters of the amendment could not have intended a fundamental change in the structure of power—that he does not even seem to notice the illogic of his position. (As an aside, I would like to point out the recurrence of fictions about "intent." I have described in this book how Black, Marshall, Taney, and Miller have written such fictions. So long as judges need to ask—what were they trying to do when they wrote—then so long will such dangerous fictions be written.)

The consequence of *Slaughterhouse* is that equality, as a norm of our constitutional law, is not a norm of equal citizenship, and so the action had to move elsewhere. I have set forth the details, since most people do not know that *Slaughterhouse* preserved the dual citizenship theory of *Dred Scott*. However, most people are aware of the broad outlines of what happened next. The Fourteenth Amendment states that "no state shall . . . deny to any person within its jurisdiction the equal protection of the law." Three decades after the end of the Civil War, the Supreme Court decided *Plessy v. Ferguson*,[13] which undermined the Fourteenth Amendment's guarantee of equality. *Plessy* challenged a Louisiana statute that required railroads to "provide equal but separate accommodations for the white and colored races" and made it a misdemeanor for anyone to go "into a coach or compartment to which by race he does not belong." The Supreme Court upheld the statute; segregation became the norm in the South (and beyond); *Plessy* remained the governing precedent until 1954, when the Supreme Court decided *Brown v. Board of Education*.[14] After *Brown*, judges began to discuss how the norm of equality might be incorporated into constitutional law. I shall not try to describe these legal developments; instead, I wish to address an aspect of the developments that intersect with the theme of this book. My question is, "How were the stories that I have described—

13. 163 U.S. 537 (1896).
14. 347 U.S. 483 (1954).

the *Marbury* story of limits, and the *McCulloch* story of growth—used in this context?"

Of course, so long as there are no fundamental conflicts among the judges, there will be no fights over which story to tell. Stories are used to persuade, and so the judges do not need to fight over which story is best until they begin to disagree about the substantive content of the equality norm. Furthermore, passion in storytelling is most likely to be aroused when disagreement is about whether there should be a change of course, a retreat, or a new direction. The key transition case, which symbolizes the changes that new judges can bring to a court, is *San Antonio Independent School District v. Rodriguez,*[15] which was decided in 1973. Unfortunately for my thesis, the complications of that case detract from its value as an example. The case involved school finance; the claim was that the Texas system of financing public schools had led to great inequalities of resources among the school districts in the state. The court rejected the claim in a close vote, 5–4, and in retrospect, we interpret *Rodriguez* as marking a new era of uncertainty and vacillation. In the mid- to late 1960s, one might have characterized the Court as having a confident vision of the future. By the seventies, one might best have characterized the Court as split and drifting. But at the time, many of us discounted the significance of *Rodriguez* because we imagined that it was merely the peculiar difficulties of school finance that led the justices to hesitate, to abstain. In retrospect, *Rodriguez* symbolizes a significant retreat by the Court from its activist stance. In time, the hesitations of the seventies were replaced with the new directions of the eighties. I would like now to discuss a case decided in 1989, which symbolizes rather nicely the new era, and which contains a split in the stories that are told.

III

In the *City of Richmond v. J. A. Croson Co.*[16] the Supreme Court held unconstitutional a minority-business set-aside established in the city of Richmond, Virginia. Under the Richmond plan, the general contractors doing construction for the city were required to set aside thirty percent of the value of their subcontracts for minority-owned businesses. The Supreme

15. 411 U.S. 1 (1973).
16. 488 U.S. 469 (1989).

Court held this plan unconstitutional by a vote of six to three. The issue provoked eighty-six pages of opinion, with four of the six in the majority and two of the three judges in the minority publishing their views. The legal dialectics in the opinion were centered around two issues, which I might characterize as instructions from the Supreme Court to legislators and instructions from the Supreme Court to the judiciary. Legislators were told *when* they could use a racial classification in a statute; the judiciary were told *how* they should review such classifications. Legislators were told that they could legislate with reference to race only when they were attempting to remedy past discrimination. Judges were told that they should review all such legislation *very carefully*, imposing strict standards of justification. The context for these legal issues was two precedents of the Supreme Court. In *Fullilove v. Klutznick*[17] the Supreme Court sustained a minority-business set-aside established by act of Congress. In *Wygant v. Jackson Board of Education*[18] the Supreme Court struck down a school board's program to set aside a certain number of teaching positions for minority teachers. As one can imagine, if the justices thought that the *Croson* case was like *Fullilove*, then the Richmond ordinance is valid, but if they thought it was like *Wygant*, then it was invalid.

The *Croson* case is now regarded as the controlling precedent on the power of state and local governments to set up race-conscious programs. As a practical matter, the case tightens up the requirements. Needless to say, the six opinions are complicated and complex. At the risk of oversimplifying them, I shall focus on the stories that lie behind the complexities. I would like to start by focusing on the lead opinion for the majority, which was written by Justice O'Connor, and the lead opinion for the dissenters, which was written by Justice Marshall. I wish to contend that Sandra Day O'Connor's opinion is like *Marbury* and that Thurgood Marshall's opinion is like *McCulloch*. Of course, the fit will not be perfect, but there is enough substance to the comparison to reveal something crucial about our legal culture.

O'Connor begins by describing the dispute as a conflict between two principles: "In this case, we confront once again the tension between the Fourteenth Amendment's guarantee of equal treatment to all citizens, and the use of race-based measures to ameliorate the effects of past discrimination" (*Croson*, 476–77). Marshall's first sentence begins with a historical

17. 448 U.S. 448 (1980).
18. 476 U.S. 267 (1986).

reference: "It is a welcome symbol of racial progress when the former capital of the Confederacy acts forthrightly to confront the effects of racial discrimination in its midst" (528). This contrast between law and history as the starting point in the first sentence (a contrast that evokes the differing openings of *Marbury* and *McCulloch*) shapes much of what follows.

In both opinions, this initial peroration is followed by a description of the facts in the particular case. Since Justice O'Connor has identified the issue as a conflict between two legal principles, she quite naturally begins her statement of facts with a focus on certain details. Her statement begins with April 11, 1983, the date on which the Richmond City Council adopted its plan (477). In the next two pages she describes the legal essentials of the plan, and in the following two, the hearings before the city council. There next follows a statement of the rejection of Croson's bid to install plumbing fixtures at the city jail, which bid was rejected because he did not comply with the minority set-aside for his subcontractors (481–83), and the subsequent litigation of the issue in the district court and the court of appeals (483–86). One might characterize O'Connor's focus as either "precise" or "narrow," depending on how one evaluates it. Justice Marshall, as one might guess, preferred the latter characterization: "As an initial matter, the majority takes an exceedingly myopic view of the factual predicate on which the Richmond city council relied. . . . The majority analyzes Richmond's initiative as if it were based solely upon the facts about local construction and contracting practices adduced during the city council session at which the measure was enacted" (530).

The key sentence in O'Connor's description of the facts is the following: "There was no direct evidence of race discrimination on the part of the city in letting contracts or any evidence that the city's prime contractors had discriminated against minority owned subcontractors" (480). O'Connor is not claiming that such discrimination (either by the city or the contractors) did not exist; she is complaining that there was no such evidence presented to the city council. Why is this observation relevant? The hidden premise is that a city council (with respect to matters of race) should act like a court; judicial action is justified only if it is supported by evidence in the record. O'Connor is imposing the same requirement for making a record on the city council. Of course, a city council need not act like a court with regard to all of the issues before it. It can take money from citizens' pockets by way of taxation without justifying the details by evidence on the record; it can decide to outlaw firecrackers and permit pistols without supporting the distinction. Most of us would agree, I think, that the distinction between spending public money in a race-conscious way is different from deciding which alkaloids (tobacco, coffee, alcohol, marijuana, cocaine) should be permitted. But why should the difference generate a requirement that there be evidence submitted directly to the city council?

Justice Marshall thought that to focus on the evidence presented to the city council was to ask the wrong question. Marshall starts with the national evidence, not the Richmond evidence. In 1977, Congress established the construction set-aside that was sustained in *Fullilove*. This action was not supported by findings on a record, since the set-aside was adopted by floor amendment. However, there had been federal studies, so the Court in *Fullilove* assumed that these floor amendments were based on the preexisting studies, which were a 1975 report by the United States Commission on Civil Rights and 1975 and 1977 reports by the House Committee on Small Business. These reports documented racial discrimination in the construction market. Furthermore, Marshall points out that both the House and Senate small business committees have issued reports subsequent to 1977 that have continued to document discrimination (530–33).

Given the national evidence, it is enough for Marshall that there was testimony in the record before the city council that referred to the national evidence and stated Richmond was no different. In short, Marshall and O'Connor are asking radically different questions of the evidence before the council. O'Connor is asking, Did the evidence before the city council prove discrimination in the construction industry in Richmond? Marshall is asking, Given that discrimination in the construction industry is pervasive throughout the nation, does the evidence before the Richmond City Council prove that Richmond is an exception? Once the question is stated, the answers are relatively obvious; the answer to each question is no. Consequently, the problem is, Which question should be asked?

Which story one should tell depends on the background story that one assumes should characterize normal life. Is normal life a world of racial discrimination, or not? I do not wish to reach for the rather easy answer to the question about normality, since the peculiar legal context of the problem is more complicated than that. The more precise question is, What sort of story do we wish to have told in court? And in that context, what will be the background and what will be the exception? The stories that are told in court need not, and probably should not, make the same background assumptions that historians and social scientists would make in their discourse outside court. When we leave the world of the historian and enter the courtroom dialectic of lawyers, we must be alert to the problems and traditions of the law. Whenever one tells a story in court, one necessarily speaks against a background of assumptions—that bullets kill, that water runs downhill, and so forth. One could never prove anything within the practical limitations set by the clock and the bank unless the proof can proceed on the basis of certain common understandings. For the most part, we make these assumptions without even being explicit, but occasionally, lawyers are explicit about what must be proved as distinguished from what may be taken for granted, and the technical tool for being explicit is called "the burden of proof." For example, in a criminal case one says that the prosecution has the burden of proof to establish both the corpus delicti and the criminal agency, these being fancy phrases that mean the prosecution must prove both that a crime was committed and that the defendant did it. We do not accept as a background fact, for which we can dispense with evidence and proof, that a crime was committed or that the defendant did it, and as this example suggests, our traditions about what needs to be proved rests on assumptions that are not solely statistical but are also political and ethical in their content.

I have made this apparent digression into the burden of proof because I think it highly relevant to understanding O'Connor's opinion. At one level of analysis, her opinion seems absurd. Why would anyone assume that discrimination in the construction industry in Richmond, Virginia, is more likely to be the exception than the norm? O'Connor's position seems to rest on such an assertion, and it is hard to take this assumption seriously. But at another level, her making this assumption is not surprising at all, and indeed, it fits well with the legal tradition, which of course, may only be proof about the limitations of the law. Step back and try to rerun the legal dialectics through one's imagination. Let us declare that our civil rights include the right not to be discriminated against on the grounds of race. If we have such rights, then those who do discriminate have done something wrong. We have civil rights, which can be violated by civil wrongs. In ordinary legal discourse, we use the word "torts" as the category for civil wrongs; the word "tort" derives from the French language and its survival in our legal discourse is one of the residual consequences of the Norman conquest of England. If the civil wrong of discrimination is a tort, for which one can sue as a plaintiff, then naturally enough the judges who handle the lawsuits for this new tort will assimilate it to the existing body of tort law (to rethink everything from scratch is not the way of the judiciary). These judges look around in the rummage heap of torts to find something that looks like the civil wrong of discrimination. Having looked for an analogy, the judges have concluded that the tort of discrimination looks like such intentional torts as assault, battery, false imprisonment, trespass, and so forth. If a plaintiff is to gain redress for a battery, the plaintiff must prove that he or she has been struck, that the striking was intentional, and that this offensive contact was neither privileged nor consented to. By analogy, so too for discrimination.

By the way, I have used the example of battery because of its historical relevance to the topic of equality. Dred Scott began his case in federal court as a battery case, claiming that he had been unlawfully touched by the defendant, to which the response was made that the touching was lawful since Dred Scott was a slave and a master is permitted to lay hands on a slave.[19] The common law of battery was thus used as a technique for adjudicating the status of free or slave. But as you know, the case failed because the Supreme Court held that the trial court (then known as the circuit court) did not have jurisdiction: a federal court does not have jurisdiction over battery cases unless there is diversity of citizenship; but there can be no diversity of citizenship unless both parties are citizens; and Dred Scott was not eligible, according to the Supreme Court, to this status, since his ancestors were African and he was consequently either a free descendant of slaves, or else a slave himself, and neither was eligible to be a citizen.

Once we have entered the legal discourse of intentional torts, then it follows that the customary rules about burden of proof must be employed. Thus O'Connor's focus on how much evidence was presented to the city council becomes more understandable in the context of legal culture. Since discrimination is a tort, just as assault and battery is a tort, and since Justice O'Connnor has ruled that state and local governments cannot use racial classifications unless they are acting to remedy past discrimination, certain consequences follow. If discrimination is a tort, and if local government can only act to remedy the tort, then we must be sure that the tort has occurred. If local government's job is to remedy this sort of wrong, then its job resembles the job that courts have, and it seems to follow (if one is reasoning by analogy) that the city council should act like a court. No court would judge that discrimination has occurred unless evidence is presented on the record, and so O'Connor concludes that a city council should do likewise. Within the context of a certain type of legal culture, every step in the argument makes sense. Consequently, we should ask of O'Connor's

19. See Don E. Fehrenbacher, *The Dred Scott Case* (New York: Oxford University Press, 1978), and Walter Ehrlich, *They Have No Rights* (Westport, Conn.: Greenwood Press, 1979).

opinion not the easy question about its social understanding, but the harder question about its assumed legal world. Why is it that judges have adopted the discourse of intentional torts to tell stories in court about racial discrimination? In order to understand why, we need to take a closer look at O'Connor's opinion. As I have already stated, she begins with a statement that the case involves the clash between two fundamental principles, the "guarantee of equal treatment to all citizens" and "the use of race-based measures to ameliorate the effects of past discrimination" (*Croson*, 476–77). Then in part 1 of the opinion she states the facts by giving a history of the ordinance, followed by a history of J. A. Croson Company's bid on a contract and a history of the litigation in the lower courts. As I said earlier, the key sentence in her statement of facts is the observation that there was "no direct evidence" about discrimination in the construction industry (480).

Let us now pick up O'Connor's opinion with part 2 as she begins to address the legal issues. She begins part 2 as she began the opinion itself, with a story of conflict. Part 1 began with a tension between two legal principles; part 2 begins with a conflict between the parties: "The parties and their supporting *amici* fight an initial battle over the scope of the city's power to adopt legislation designed to address the effects of past discrimination" (486). The alternatives are that the city may use race-conscious remedies only when it is correcting its own prior discrimination, a proposition that might rest on the *Wygant* case, and the proposition that the city enjoys the same sort of power that was approved for the Congress in *Fullilove*. Let me quote Justice O'Connor's description of these alternatives. As she states it, the choice is between the argument "that the city must limit any race-based remedial efforts to eradicating of effects of its own prior discrimination" versus the position that "the city of Richmond enjoys sweeping legislative power to define and attack the effects of prior discrimination in its local construction industry" (486). Judges often like to flatter themselves as being wise enough to find the reasonable middle ground between two extremes. In this case, Justice O'Connor executes this ritual: "We find that neither of these two rather stark alternatives can withstand analysis" (486).

Why does O'Connor think that the two alternatives are "stark"? Why would it be extreme to give the Richmond City Council the sort of power that Congress exercised in *Fullilove*? O'Connor does not say; but we can infer it from her subsequent discussion. She immediately turns to a discussion of the *Fullilove* case. She describes the case and the opinion of the former chief justice Warren Burger. O'Connor interprets Burger's opinion in *Fullilove* to rest on the powers of Congress to enforce the Fourteenth Amendment, a power explicitly granted to it in Section 5 of the Fourteenth Amendment. Consequently, she asserts that there is a sound textual basis for distinguishing the United States Congress from the city council of Richmond: the Fourteenth Amendment explicitly grants a power to Congress that it does not grant to state legislators or city council members. But as one reads the crucial pages in the opinion (486–92), one discerns that O'Connor's opinion rests on more than the textual features of the Fourteenth Amendment. For example, she notes that Burger did not apply a strict scrutiny test or any other rigorous test in judging the constitutionality of the congressionally mandated set-aside. Instead, Burger said that the courts must defer to congressional judgments (487). In deferring to congressional judgment, there are two separate matters about which a court might accept Congress's judgment: the facts and their appropriate remedies. Burger's opinion that the judiciary should defer to congressional judgment on the facts, that is, their conclusion that there had been racial discrimination in the construction industry, was routine; consequently, O'Connor does not emphasize that part of Burger's opinion. Instead, she asks, Assuming that there was discrimination in the construction industry, what is the appropriate remedy? Is a set-aside an appropriate remedy? Burger's opinion makes clear that congressional power is greater than judicial power on the question of remedy, and so O'Connor quotes what she judges to be the crucial language, italicizing what she wishes to emphasize: "Here we deal . . . not with the limited remedial powers of a federal court, for example, but with the broad remedial powers of Congress. It is fundamental that *in no organ of government, state or federal, does there repose a more comprehensive remedial power than in the Congress,* expressly charged by the Constitution with competence and authority to enforce equal protection guarantees" (488).

The legal consequences of Burger's summary of congressional power are not limited to the language that Burger used. Perhaps even more important are the cases that Burger cites. She notes (at 487) that Burger rested his decision on the precedent of *Katzenbach v. Morgan,*[20] and if one turns to that case, one can read that congressional power to enforce the Fourteenth Amendment has the same broad scope that John Marshall gave the Congress in *McCulloch v. Maryland.* In short, the question reduces itself to the relevance of *McCulloch.* Will the Congress, state legislators, and city councils have the power to adapt the equal protection guarantee to events? The precedents say yes, so far as Congress is concerned; but O'Connor draws

20. *Katzenbach v. Morgan,* 384 U.S. 641, 650–51 (1966).

the line there: "To hold otherwise would be to cede control over the content of the Equal Protection Clause to the 50 state legislators and their myriad political subdivisions" (*Croson*, 490). The consequence of ceding control is one that O'Connor finds unacceptable: "The Framers of the Fourteenth Amendment . . . [intended] to place clear limits on the States' use of race as a criterion for legislative action, and to have the federal courts enforce those limitations" (491). In short, O'Connor's fundamental desire is to find a way to constrain the power of state and local government, and she employs the technical device of requiring evidence to be presented at a hearing as a means toward that end. Note how the several different parts of O'Connor's opinion fit together: she assumes that racial discrimination is a tort; she asserts that the city government can act to correct such wrongs, but before it can act, it must have evidence presented to it that such wrongs have been committed; and she asserts that the Fourteenth Amendment is intended to place limits on state and local government. The legal analysis—the vocabulary of torts and evidence—provides the tools by which the overarching desire to set limits can be executed. State governments can correct wrongs, but they are not empowered to do more.

As you can imagine, Justice Marshall has a response to this line of argument (557–61). Let me paraphrase it. The grant of a positive power to the Congress should not be read as implying a negation of state power. The grant of a power to Congress was necessary, since the whole field of civil rights was beyond congressional jurisdiction prior to the Civil War amendments. However, the law was clear that prior to these amendments, the states did have power over civil rights. Consequently, it was necessary to grant a power to Congress; it was not necessary to grant any power to the states. I might further add, as a supplement to Marshall's argument, that the Congress itself is subject to the prohibitions of Section 1: the Congress may not deprive any person of equal protection of the laws.[21] Consequently, it is a plausible, albeit not necessary, interpretation of the Constitution that all levels of government (when acting within the scope of their jurisdiction) are both prohibited from denying equal protection and empowered to enforce this guarantee. In the case of a conflict between a city council ordinance and a congressional statute, the supremacy clause would say that congressional power is the trump; but if there is no conflict between state and federal law, one could say that all levels of government are empowered to act.

21. *Bolling v. Sharpe*, 347 U.S. 497 (1954).

Marshall's real passion in his opinion is unleashed by something more than the legal dynamics. At the level of legal analysis, he argues that the majority errs, and in parts 1 and 2 of his opinion (*Croson*, 530–51), he argues that the precedents can and should be construed to sustain what the Richmond City Council has done. He then moves beyond this legal dialectics and contests the majority's vision of the Constitution: "I would ordinarily end my analysis at this point. . . . However, I am compelled to add more . . ." (551). Marshall feels "compelled to add more" because he believes that the *Croson* majority has turned away from the path of the law to which he had devoted so much of his life.

Recall that there were two basic legal issues: What can legislatures do? And how should judges review what they have done? The second question— how to review—resists any simple analysis. There is some jargon that the legal community uses—"rational basis," "intermediate standard," "strict scrutiny"—but the meanings of these phrases shift in subtle ways from judge to judge, from decade to decade. Despite these obscurities, everyone agrees that the so-called strict scrutiny test requires a judge to put the burden of proof on the state to defend the statute, and furthermore, the test makes it hard for the state's defense to win. As one can well imagine, Marshall was disturbed, outraged, that the majority used "strict scrutiny" to review what the Richmond City Council had done. He asserted that there was an obvious difference (moral, historical, constitutional) between hostile, racist legislation and legislation that attempted to remedy past discrimination. Marshall argued his position at length (551–61), but the following paragraph perhaps captures the flavor of his response:

In concluding that remedial classifications warrant no different standard of review under the Constitution than the most brutal and repugnant forms of state-sponsored racism, a majority of this Court signals that it regards racial discrimination as largely a phenomenon of the past, and that government bodies need no longer preoccupy themselves with rectifying racial injustice. I, however, do not believe this Nation is anywhere close to eradicating racial discrimination or its vestiges. In constitutionalizing its wishful thinking, the majority today does a grave disservice not only to those victims of past and present racial discrimination in this Nation whom government has long sought to assist, but also to this Court's long tradition of approaching issues of race with the utmost sensitivity. (552–53)

Marshall's eloquent and powerful rhetoric attacks the majority on two levels, for being ignorant of social reality, and for abandoning the Court's historic role. He repeats the latter charge of abandonment at the end of his dissent: "The majority today sounds a full-scale retreat from the Court's longstanding solicitude to race-conscious remedial efforts 'directed toward deliverance of the century-old promise of equality of economic opportunity.'"[22]

The most fascinating feature of Marshall's powerful rhetoric is his assertion that the Supreme Court has a "long tradition of approaching issues of race with the utmost sensitivity" and that the *Croson* decision represents a "full-scale retreat" from this "longstanding solicitude." Marshall has a vision of a nation in which discrimination has been, and still is, pervasive, and yet this nation has a Supreme Court that is ever solicitous and sensitive in racial matters. How could this be, one wonders? How could it be that the justices have escaped being contaminated by the discrimination so rampant in the nation? How have they evaded absorbing the poison? One suspects that Marshall knew all too well that this rhetoric of a hostile nation and a sympathetic Court might tip toward fiction. One suspects that Marshall understood far better than we just how insensitive and unsolicitous his colleagues were in racial matters.

So let us conclude that Marshall knew that the "Court" he described was an abstraction and a fiction. When Marshall attributes to this "Court" a wisdom and compassion that he knows quite well are lacking in his colleagues, he knows, in one corner of his mind, he is writing a fiction, yet in another, perhaps he doesn't; it is hard to tell a story and not somehow believe it. Marshall has a vision of what the law could be, and like most of us, he finds it natural to cast his vision into a story, and once he is caught up in this story of what the law could be, the blurry edges between fiction and fact become even more blurred, and the story of what could be starts to become the story of what has been.

IV

As Chief Justice John Marshall once said, in a passage I have previously quoted, it is *"a constitution"* that we must expound, and as he also noted, a constitution both grants power and limits it. But where should the empha-

---

22. *Croson*, 561. Marshall is quoting *Fullilove*, 463.

sis lie? On the limit or on the grant? And the Fourteenth Amendment poses the question as sharply as does any other part of the Constitution, since it simultaneously limits and grants with respect to equality. Sandra Day O'Connor saw great public danger in racial classifications, and so she emphasized the limits. Thurgood Marshall saw a great need to overcome the effects of past discrimination, and so he emphasized the power. For the day, and for the near future, we can say that the constitution of limits has prevailed, but I would not venture a guess about more distant futures, nor would I imagine that the members of the Court will be consistent in the future with the precedent of the *Croson* case.

And most of all, I do not wish to impose closure on this debate between limits and powers. I do not suggest that we should choose between *Marbury* and *McCulloch*. In some way or another, we will, as I suppose we must, continue to believe in both of these cases and continue to use both as precedents. However, honoring both cases does make it hard to tell coherent stories about the law. When we talk about race and equal protection, *Marbury* doesn't work because the notion of unchanging limits is contradicted by the facts of change, and the *McCulloch* story of growth doesn't work because the change seems so chaotic, with as much backsliding as forward motion. In 1776, the Declaration of Independence spoke of equality, yet many of its signers knew that their actions were suspect under these principles. In 1787, the Constitution spoke ambiguously, and in 1857 Chief Justice Taney tried to exploit the ambiguity to banish the norm of equality, whereas Lincoln tried to keep it alive. The Civil War amendments brought the norm of equality into the Constitution, but in 1873 in *Slaughterhouse*, the Supreme Court began to "interpret" equality back out of it and completed this process in 1896 in *Plessy v. Ferguson*. In 1954, *Brown* revived the norm of equality, but *Rodriguez* in 1973 marked a halt to activism, and *Croson* in 1989 displayed sharp division over the constitutional limits on power and the constitutional grants of power. It is hard for me to interpret such erratic change as "growth."

5

What Stories Should
We Tell?

Throughout the preceding chapters, I have described the two basic stories—the story of limits and the story of growth—and I have tried to separate the factual from the fictional in each. And I have also tried to show how a story can be false despite being factual or true despite being fictional. It is now appropriate to move away from description to evaluation. Let us now leave behind the problems of church and state and racial equality and look at the problem of storytelling. What standards should we have? How should we evaluate and criticize stories? What is wrong with the stories of limit and growth?

1

There is an implied criticism in what I have already written. As I have gone along, I have criticized, but let me now summarize why one might be uncomfortable with the stories of *Marbury* and *McCulloch*. The *Marbury* story seems implausible, indeed, even impossible. The thesis that the Constitution establishes an unchanging law that is beyond the power of the political world to alter is surely false. One hardly knows where to begin in listing the objections. The document is too short; it doesn't contain enough detail; if it does establish some unchanging law, then it doesn't establish very much of it. Another objection is even more important, which is, that the judges are not isolated from their culture; they too are born into families, study in schools, work in an economy. Consequently, since the culture changes, and is always diverse, we get judges who have absorbed values that differ from those of their predecessors. Different judges produce different decisions. One cannot repeat too often the basic proposition that different judges will decide cases differently, assuming, that is, that the differences are not minor idiosyncrasies of personality but basic differences in social values. Given these differences, an unchanging constitution is impossible.

If Marshall made a promise in *Marbury*, then that promise has not been kept; the judiciary has not kept the constitutional law of the nation unchanged. Each generation has introduced change, sometimes small, sometimes large. Indeed, if we were to pick a sample of important cases from a decade, sum up the constitutional law that those cases establish, and then move forward three or four decades and repeat the exercise, we would find a mix of continuity and discontinuity; some cases from the early period would still be honored in the latter; some would not. Furthermore, if we were to repeat the exercise for different decades, the ratio of continuity and discontinuity would itself change. In short, although John Marshall was right in saying that if the Congress were final in determining what statutes were constitutional, then the Congress could change the Constitution by the ordinary process of enacting a statute, he failed to state the corollary of this obvious truth. The corollary is that if the Supreme Court is final, then it can change the Constitution by the ordinary process of deciding a case. And of course, it has.

If the *Marbury* story of stasis won't work, what about the *McCulloch* story of growth? The *McCulloch* story looks closer to being right, in that it is true that change has occurred, but even so, this story too is deceptive. As told in that case, the change is a triumphal march. The nation's destiny is to extend from the St. Croix to the Gulf of Mexico, from the Atlantic to the Pacific, and throughout this terrain of growth and movement, power must follow. Depending on who you are, the story is either inspiring or chilling. The Native Americans, as one can imagine, tend not to find it inspiring.

Our neighbors in Canada and Mexico also have their difficulties with it. The growth of power is not always a benign and happy phenomenon.

John Marshall wrote his story about triumphal growth and progress in 1819. One year before that Keats wrote a less sanguine account.

> I was at home,
> And should have been most happy—but I saw
> Too far into the sea; where every maw
> The greater on the less feeds evermore;—
> But I saw too distinct into the core
> Of an eternal fierce destruction,
> And so from Happiness I far was gone.
> Still am I sick of it: and though to-day
> I've gathered young spring-leaves, and flowers gay
> Of Periwinkle and wild strawberry,
> Still do I that most fierce destruction see,
> The shark at savage prey—the hawk at pounce,
> The gentle Robin, like a pard or ounce,
> Ravening a worm. [1]

One of the curious variants of the growth story can be found in those who see the story of our constitutional law to be the story of the growth of liberty. The franchise has been extended, the scope of free speech has been enlarged, and so forth. But of course, what you find depends on where you look. It is true that the franchise has been extended, but the power of individual voters has been diminished, and since voters are not fools, their rate of participation in elections has fallen off; they know that the elections are less important than they once were. (This topic of diminished citizen power is complex, and I cannot begin to summarize it. Let me say simply that the growth of federal power vis-à-vis the states, and then the growth of judicial and administrative power within the federal scheme has functioned to diminish citizen power.)

The modern federal judiciary will act to protect First Amendment rights of speech and press, whereas formerly one was dependent on state judiciaries to protect these rights, but it is not so clear that we should describe this change as the growth of free speech and a free press. Freedom of the press

1. John Keats, "To J. H. Reynolds, Esq." in *The Oxford Authors*, ed. Elizabeth Cook (Oxford: Oxford University Press, 1990), 184–85.

has always belonged to whoever owns the press. Furthermore, the press itself has become the mass media, and the scope of discourse via the contemporary mass media does not seem broader than the diversity of views promulgated in the era that preceded the mass media. As for the individual speaker, what access does an individual have now to the public forum? Where is the public forum? What is it? There are no quick and easy answers to the questions, or if there are, I don't know them. Furthermore, any answer that one might give would be a historical answer, and as all well know, the computer and computer networks are currently generating technical changes that will produce, for better or worse, a totally different configuration of power and opportunity for free speech and free press. For the moment, there is no constitutional law of computer networks, and no one knows whether any will ever develop; if such a law of computer networks were to develop, no one knows what it might turn out to be. Consequently, I think that it would be silly to tell the story as one of growth, of the flourishing of liberty.

Perhaps the most subtle error in the *McCulloch* story is an error hidden in the metaphor of growth. In this metaphor, the "law" is assumed to be an organism that grows. I have already quoted Holmes's famous sentence from his treatise, "The life of the law has not been logic; it has been experience," and I have quoted his use of the same metaphor in *Missouri v. Holland*, the case involving migratory birds. I wish to emphasize the hidden metaphor in the phrase "the life of the law," since that phrase and that metaphor seem capable of generating the most subtle and grievous of errors. In this metaphor, the law is made into a thing (reification) and this thing is given life (personification). However, the law is a set of norms that ought to guide, and sometimes does guide, human action. A set of diverse and complex norms is not a single thing (and thus reification is an error), and moreover, a set of norms does not have a life of its own, but depends upon the vagaries of human knowledge and will (and thus personification is an even graver error).

Aside from the errors of reification and personification, the metaphors of growth also imply the metaphor of "development" (youth and maturity) and "trends," similar to those found in the non-Darwinian schemes of evolution that I criticized in Chapter 1. But change in law is not growth. Some norms drop out, others are added, and the norms in general are subtly changed by being applied to new circumstances. I don't have any simple proposals for understanding this complex phenomenon, but I insist that the metaphor of "growth" is singularly inept.

For all of these reasons, we should doubt that *Marbury* and *McCulloch* are good models of storytelling. If we are to do law at all, we will need to tell stories, and those stories will necessarily be fictional in part, but these particular fictions are objectionable. So how shall we choose among fictions?

II

The best stories to tell are those which are most nearly true, even though they are fictional, but alas, to say that is to deepen our difficulties, not lessen them. Recall that the central meaning of the word "fiction," as used throughout this book, is that a fiction is discourse produced by the imagination and is not necessarily based on fact. If a story is imagined and nonfactual, how can it be true? The difficulty here is caused by the obscure metaphor "based on." What can it possibly mean when we say that a story is or is not "based on" facts? This metaphor evokes startlingly inept images: the base of a pedestal, the foundation of a house. We imagine a base holding up the structure which arises above it, or conversely, a structure standing on the base, like the horse and rider of an equestrian statue standing on the pedestal.

These converse relations of "holding up" and "standing on" are physical relations in which two parts touch. By analogy, a story "based on" facts would be a story that "touched" the facts, that "stood on" the facts, in the right sort of way. This metaphor can mislead us. Perhaps it would be helpful if we note that this metaphor of "holding up" and "standing on" doesn't work well with theories either. Good theories, like good stories, have a complicated and indirect relationship to facts. Theoretical terms (for example, "mass" or "energy") do not match up with facts in any straightforward way. And by analogy, I would suggest that good stories, like good theories, are indirectly linked, often by devious routes, to the facts.

Willard Van Orman Quine has tried to explain how theories do not "touch" the facts.

> What, in other words, is the nature of the relation between a statement and the experiences which contribute to or detract from its confirmation?
>
> The most naive view of the relation is that it is one of direct report. This is *radical reductionism*. Every meaningful statement is held

to be translatable into a statement (true or false) about immediate experience. . . .

The dogma of reductionism survives in the supposition that each statement, taken in isolation from its fellows, can admit of confirmation or information at all. My counter suggestion, issuing essentially from Carnap's doctrine of the physical world in the *Aufbau*, is that our statements about the external world face the tribunal of sense experience not individually but only as a corporate body. . . .

The totality of our so-called knowledge or beliefs, from the most casual matters of geography and history to the profoundest laws of atomic physics or even of pure mathematics and logic, is a man-made fabric which impinges on experience only along the edges. Or, to change the figure, total science is like a field of force whose boundary conditions are experience. A conflict with experience at the periphery occasions readjustments in the interior of the field. Truth values have to be redistributed over some of our statements. Reevaluation of some statements entails reevaluation of others, because of their logical interconnections—the logical laws being in turn simply certain further statements of the system, certain further elements of the field. Having reevaluated one statement we must reevaluate some others, which may be statements logically connected with the first or may be the statements of logical connections themselves. But the total field is so underdetermined by its boundary conditions, experience, that there is much latitude of choice as to what statements to reevaluate in the light of any single contrary experience. No particular experiences are linked with any particular statements in the interior of the field, except indirectly through considerations of equilibrium affecting the field as a whole.

If this view is right, it is misleading to speak of the empirical content of an individual statement—especially if it is a statement at all remote from the experiential periphery of the field. Furthermore it becomes folly to seek a boundary between synthetic statements, which hold contingently on experience, and analytic statements, which hold come what may. Any statement can be held true come what may, if we make drastic enough adjustments elsewhere in the system. Even a statement very close to the periphery can be held true in the face of recalcitrant experience by pleading hallucination or by amending certain statements of the kind called logical laws. Conversely, by the same token, no statement is immune to revision.

Revision even of the logical laws of the excluded middle has been proposed as a means of simplifying quantum mechanics; and what difference is there in principle between such a shift and the shift whereby Kepler superseded Ptolemy, or Einstein Newton, or Darwin Aristotle?[2]

If Quine is right about theories, then good theories may relate to facts in a way analogous to how stories relate to facts. We can examine this analogy by reviewing how stories are used in trials. Perhaps lawyers and jurors use stories in the same way that scientists use theories: to organize facts, to generate questions, to evaluate alternative assertions, and so forth.

In *Reconstructing Reality in the Courtroom*, Lance Bennett and Martha Feldman examine the process of proof at trial in some sixty different criminal trials. They conclude that the best way to make sense about what is going on is to say that the opposing lawyers are trying to present alternative stories. Each story offers a way of accounting for the facts; the jury's task is to decide which story fits the facts better. Bennett and Feldman suggest that there are several advantages for the legal system when lawyers use stories, one of the most significant being that lay participants in the trial can understand what is going on if stories are told. Furthermore, by casting the evidence within the structure of a story, one is able to cope with the disjointed presentation of the evidence. Indeed, a literary critic who reads Bennett and Feldman might be inclined to say that a trial resembles an experimental novel, although Bennett and Feldman put the matter rather more conservatively.

Not only do stories make it possible to organize large amounts of information in coherent fashion, they are ideally suited to organizing information in the way in which it is presented in trials. Once the basic plot outline of a story begins to emerge it is possible to integrate information that is presented in the form of subplots, time disjunctures, or multiple perspectives on the same scene. Readers of novels and viewers of movies are familiar with literary devices such as flashbacks, flash-forwards, subplots, and multiple points of view. As long as a plot outline can be constructed at some point, it is possible to assimilate such disjointed information into a coherent framework. In trials cases often unfold in a more complex and disjointed fashion

2. Willard Van Orman Quine, "Two Dogmas of Empiricism," in *From a Logical Point of View* (New York: Harper & Row, 1963), 38, 41,42–43.

than do plots in novels or movies. The juror or spectator in a trial may be confronted with conflicting testimony, disorienting time lapses, the piecemeal reconstruction of a scene from the perspectives of many witnesses and experts, and a confusing array of subplots. Without the aid of an analytical device such as the story, the disjointed presentations of information in trials would be difficult, if not impossible, to assimilate.[3]

Nancy Pennington and Reid Hastie have examined how jurors use stories. Their research project is not yet complete, and indeed, their research project is a more difficult one than Bennett and Feldman undertook. Bennett and Feldman were interested in what lawyers did; Pennington and Hastie want to know how jurors think, and their hypothesis is that jurors use stories to think about the evidence. Their technique has been to show movies of trials to their volunteers, to record their mock jurors' decisions and discussions, and then to infer from their data which hypothesis about the jury best fits the evidence.[4] One of their more interesting experimental techniques was to alter the presentation of the evidence to make it easier or harder to construct a story. The results of their experiment corroborate their hypothesis, and thus suggest that trial lawyers would be well advised to build their presentations around stories.[5]

The reader might pause and consider the analogy between how Pennington and Hastie construct their theories and how jurors construct their stories. Pennington and Hastie did a quick scan of the literature and then drew up a list of hypotheses. Their jurors listened to the opening statements and constructed alternative stories. Pennington and Hastie then devised experiments, which generated data, against which they tested their hypotheses. Their jurors listened to the testimony, against which they tested their stories. Both refined their theories or stories as they went along. Neither had a perfect match between evidence and conclusion. Both knew that there could be some other theory or story out there that they had not considered but should have. (At any rate, were I constructing a theory and story which compares social scientists and jurors, it would be something like the above.)

If the above is sound, then it follows that we must be careful in labeling

3. W. Lance Bennett and Martha S. Feldman, *Reconstructing Reality in the Courtroom* (New Brunswick: Rutgers University Press, 1981), 8–9.

4. Nancy Pennington and Reid Hastie, "A Cognitive Theory of Juror Decision Making: The Story Model," 13 *Cordozo. L. Rev.* 519 (1991).

5. Ibid., 541–44.

stories and theories as true or false. Instead, we say that some theories and stories fit the evidence better than others, that they are more or less well corroborated, and so forth. Perhaps the best way to understand this characteristic feature of our stories and theories is to refuse to characterize every possible use of true and false as a binary dichotomy, and regard them instead as the polar extremes of a continuum. We can talk about this continuum using the well-established techniques of the probability calculus or the more recent insights of fuzzy logic.[6] If I may use the jargon that is used by the theorists of the probability calculus and fuzzy logic, truth is multivalent, not bivalent. For purposes of this essay, we need not grapple with the technical details of probability and fuzzy logic; I cite them merely to make the point that it is no longer unorthodox to consider a story "more or less true." Consequently, a fiction produced by the imagination and not necessarily based on fact could *also* be more or less true, since the imagination can go beyond the facts and state what is probable, how things could have happened, and how they might happen again some day. If this conclusion is sound, then one need not dismiss all fictional stories as being necessarily false. Any fiction can have some truth in it; the question is, how much? And even more pressing, What sort of stories should we tell? And how should we tell them?

III

An evaluation of the stories that judges tell is not complete without recommendations. How should it be done? But answering this question, and advising others on how to do what they must do, is difficult. It is hard to avoid sounding like Polonius. Perhaps I can avoid the folly of propounding vague and unctuous maxims if I use a concrete example. Since I cannot "tell," with luck, I can "show." My example will be Norman Maclean's posthumous book, *Young Men and Fire.*

The subtitle of this book shows why it is an appropriate example for lawyers and judges: A *True Story of the Mann Gulch Fire.* As the subtitle indicates, Maclean is aiming to tell the truth, although he admits through-

---

6. For probability, see David A. Schum, *The Evidential Foundations of Probabilistic Reasoning* (New York: John Wiley & Sons, 1994); for fuzzy logic, see Bart Kosko, *Fuzzy Thinking: The New Science of Fuzzy Logic* (New York: Hyperion, 1993).

out that he can only present approximations and probabilities at certain key points. At law, we also aim toward the truth, although we do not regularly hit it. Furthermore, Maclean is telling the story of a particular event, the Mann Gulch fire. Lawsuits are also about particular events, and so Maclean's book offers an example that history and biography normally do not. Finally, the subtitle indicates that Maclean is aiming not merely to tell the truth, and the truth about a particular event, but a true *story* about a particular event. About one-third of the way through the book, Maclean alludes to the difference between a story and a history, and he draws the line by asserting that a storyteller must go beyond the testimony of the witnesses and try to discern those things about which they have not spoken.[7] In any contested lawsuit, lawyers and judges will have to make inferences that go beyond the evidence, and so I think we can recognize that Maclean is engaged in the same task that we are. There is, however, one distinction, but it is instructive and enlightening. For the lawyer, storytelling is not the goal. The goal is to allocate responsibility; telling the story is merely a means toward that end. For Maclean, allocating responsibility is a necessary task, but it is not the primary goal; his goal is to enlarge his understanding and to express his compassion for the young men who died. I think it is good for lawyers and judges to read this type of story in order to be instructed in what they don't do.

The Mann Gulch fire occurred about twenty miles north of Helena, Montana, adjacent to a stretch of the Missouri River known as the Gates of the Mountains. The Missouri River runs north in this area, and Captain Meriwether Lewis dubbed this stretch the Gates of the Mountains because of the spectacular and picturesque way in which the river flows at this location out of the mountains and into the plains. Mann Gulch is a dry gulch about two and a half miles long on the eastern side of the river. The southern slope of the gulch is covered by timber, the northern slope by grass and brush that were dangerously dry in the late summer fire season. The fire started when lightning hit the southern slope, and in due course it developed into the most dangerous of fires, the "blow-up." The least dangerous fire is a ground fire, in which the fire hugs the ground. A more dangerous sort of fire is the crown fire in which the fire rises to the tops of trees and jumps from treetop to treetop. But the most dangerous sort of fire, the fire in which thirteen young men died at Mann Gulch, is the blow-up, in

---

7. Norman Maclean, *Young Men and Fire: A True Story of the Mann Gulch Fire* (Chicago: University of Chicago Press, 1992), 102.

which the heat of the fire combines with the wind to generate a whirling tornado of flame that can move with the speed of the wind. There are not many who have seen one up close and lived to tell the tale. Fortunately, this type of fire is relatively rare. Unfortunately, the nature of a blow-up was little understood in 1949, and so the young men did not really know the risk that they were facing.

The plan, on August 5, 1949, was to parachute into the location of the fire, fight it all night, and be through by the next morning. Fifteen smoke jumpers parachuted in at the eastern end of the gulch, where they were joined by a firefighter on the scene, thus making the total crew sixteen in number. When they landed, the fire was down the gulch to the west of them on the southern slope, on their left as they would walk. Their foreman soon realized how dangerous this fire really was; so instead of assaulting it directly in the upper gulch, he made plans for the crew to get below it and fight it from below. In this way, they would be able to retreat to the Missouri River if necessary.

In order to get around and beneath the fire they started down the gulch on the northern slope in an attempt to get past it, but the fire crossed the gulch to the northern slope and quickly cut them off from the river. The foreman ordered his crew to retreat up the gulch, back toward where they had landed, but then the fire blew up. As it raced toward them, the foreman Wag Dodge invented on the spot something that was not then part of the Forest Service training, an escape fire. He lit a fire and called out to his men to join him in the burned-over place it was making. His orders made no sense to them, and they ran. Two made it to the top of the ridge and survived; thirteen were caught by the fire and died. Wag Dodge lay down in the space cleared by his escape fire and lived. Of the thirteen who died, eleven were dead within minutes; two lingered until noon the next day. This fire was the greatest tragedy in the history of the smoke jumpers, and on the hillside, the Forest Service has erected thirteen crosses to mark where each met his death.

How can Maclean tell this story? What more does he wish to add to this bare chronology? And what can lawyers and judges learn from his attempt? I hope to answer these questions.

The publisher's note to the book indicates that "when Maclean died in 1990 at the age of eighty-seven, *Young Men and Fire* was unfinished" (7–8). Anyone who has ever prepared a case or delivered a judgment can sympathize; time always runs out. We lack the resources, financial, intellectual, and chronological, to complete the job, to discover all of the facts, to do all of the analysis. Generally speaking, we are not as honest about this as we should be, nor do we acknowledge the inequalities of resources which make time run out sooner for some than for others. According to the publisher's note, Maclean did not start on this book until he was seventy-four. If this is so, he began gathering facts rather late; almost three decades had gone by. This gap between the time of the event and start of the inquiry is more daunting than that normally faced by lawyers and judges, but in any legal inquiry, there will be a gap, and it is always an impediment. To be sure, there was a Forest Service inquiry after the fact, but it was perhaps done too quickly, and Maclean had to seek out new sources of fact and theory (146–56). He could have done nothing without the previous investigation; but his own inquiry goes well beyond it.

In its published form, *Young Men and Fire* contains a preface and three parts. The preface, "Black Ghost," is a memoir by Maclean about first hearing about the fire back in 1949 and visiting the scene with his brother-in-law five days later. This short excerpt comprises slightly more than three percent of the total book. Part 1, which is slightly more than forty percent of the book, presents the basic story, centered around the testimony as it survived in our principal sources. Part 2 is longer, just over fifty percent of the book. It records Maclean's inquiry in which he tries to learn more about the fire in order to fill in the gaps in the basic story. Part 3 is the shortest section, less than three percent of the total. It gives us the epitome of the events.

Let us now proceed to examine Maclean's craft: How does he tell the story? Judging from the publisher's note, Maclean intended to have some sort of preface and he intended the book to be in three parts, as currently divided. Let us accept the "Black Ghost," as close enough to Maclean's own intentions and examine how the story is told. The first point to be made is that Maclean begins with the conclusion, death. One literary term for this device is *foreshadowing*. It is easy to forget, but one should not, that dramatic tension can be increased if the narrative starts with the conclusion. The tension lies in seeing the struggle against the foreshadowed death. The Greeks perfected this technique, from Homer through the great tragedians; García Marquez's *Chronicle of a Death Foretold* is a modern example of the same technique.

Having foreshadowed the terrible end, Maclean then steps back and begins chapter 1 by sketching the scene, the context, out of which the drama will grow. Chapter 1 begins:

In 1949 the smoke jumpers were not far from their origins as para-chute jumpers turned stunt performers dropping from the wings of planes at county fairs just for the hell of it plus a few dollars, less hospital expenses. By this time they were also sure they were the best fire fighters in the United States Forest Service, and although by now they were very good, especially against certain kinds of fires, they should have stopped to realize that they were newcomers in this ancient business of fighting forest fires. (19)

As these first several pages of chapter 1 develop, the arena and the context becomes a complex interweaving of the theme of youth, not merely the youth of the thirteen who would die, but the youthfulness of their occupation, of their organization, of the very technology of their equipment. Part of the tragedy is that they died so young; but youth also helped kill them, with youthful folly, youthful ignorance, and youthful inexperience making them more vulnerable.

If I may step back from Maclean's tale, I would cite here America's greatest literary theorist, Kenneth Burke. In two great works, *The Rhetoric of Motives*, and *The Grammar of Motives*, Burke opines that we explain the motives for action, and thus action itself, by contemplating the "ratios" between the basic components of an action: the actor, the act, the scene, the instruments, and the goal. These five elements of any action (which we can refer to as Burke's pentad) are part of any account of human action and can be found even at the level of a sentence. For example, "John rode downtown on his bicycle to buy a present." In this short sentence, we have the actor, John; his act, riding; the scene, the road to town; his instrument, the bicycle; and his goal, the purchase of a present. As the story implied by this sentence is developed with other sentences, as it takes its shape and presents its mysteries, any element in the pentad can come to the fore. What defects or strengths in John's character will shape the story? Will it be significant that he rode instead of walked? And what if he had gone by car instead of bicycle? Was the particular route that he took significant? And why did he go for a present instead of for food? The key to the story can be in the ratio of any one of these elements to the rest of the story, and it is possible for one who reads Burke to learn many things about the vast reper-toire of moves and turns that a storyteller can employ.

In Maclean's presentation, the theme of youth is implicated in four of the five elements of Burke's pentad. The actors were young, and so they acted with the heedlessness of the young. Jumping from planes is the sort of act that only the young can do. The instruments of their trade, parachutes and airplanes, were new. And part of the arena within which their actions are placed, the organization of smoke jumpers, was a new part of the Forest Service. Maclean has introduced the basics of his story in a way that unifies the several elements of Burke's pentad.

The fifth element in Burke's pentad is goal. In this case, the goal is to put out fires, or more specifically, to reach fires quickly by jumping in and then putting them out. The general principle is that the sooner one gets to a fire, the smaller it is; and the smaller, the easier to put out. And there is no quicker way of getting to a fire than flying in and jumping. At this point, Maclean introduces some statistics to demonstrate the utility of smoke jumping (24–26). The statistics, suitably graphed, show a random fluctuation in the number of fires, now up, now down, but with no significant pattern. However, if one also graphs the percentage of significant fires (more than ten acres burned), the statistics show a significant downward trend since World War II, and it seems fair to infer that the smoke jumpers deserve some of the credit for this downward trend in major fires. This part of chapter 1 is the first clear example of Maclean's respect for science. Unlike many of those who celebrate storytelling, Maclean does not spuriously contrast the warm liberating sweetness of stories with the cold imprisoning harshness of science. Instead, he honors science and instrumental rationality, when it is appropriate. It is wrong to risk the lives of the young in actions that are counterproductive, and so we must face honestly the question of the consequences of human action; and if one would know consequences, one must know some statistics. Maclean has written his book out of love, but he has not checked his brain at the door, since he believes that his brain can strengthen his heart, just as his heart can enlighten his brain.

At this point in the story, Maclean has covered all of the basic elements of Burke's pentad. He now takes up, as the first element to receive an extended discussion, the character of the actors. What sort of men were they? Why did they do what they did? In a short and elegant essay on this topic of character he describes what it means to be an "outfit," and further, what men get from belonging to such a group (26–33). By making his essay on character an essay on being an "outfit," Maclean shows his sure touch. I think we can all see that it is a natural move to turn to character after one has set the basic theme; the human-interest side of a story ought to come early. But it may seem strange to some that Maclean does not address the characters of these young men by presenting idiosyncratic or unique facts about their lives and personalities. To be sure, Maclean's focus may be in part driven by the availability of evidence: it is several decades after the fact, and so some of the unique details are lost forever; furthermore, the passage of time has not lessened the grief of many of the families, and Maclean is too sensitive and caring to probe at old wounds. For all of these reasons, the absence of certain details is natural. Even so, I think Maclean is right to suppose that it is the "type in general" that will engage us. What sort of person jumps out of airplanes to fight a fire? I am not now that sort of person, and perhaps I never was. But I can admire and honor them, and Maclean engages us all at that level.

Moreover, I think that lawyers would recognize that he has gone to the core of effective examination. When Maclean asks what men get out of belonging to such groups, he is asking a question that is simultaneously personal and social, he is asking about the cultural norms that can sink so deeply into a person's soul that they become part of character. We often wish to test various stories in which people say what they have done. In doing so, we ask what it would have made sense for them to have done, and this in turn includes an element of the normative, of what they ought to have done. (For an elegant study of this phenomenon, one should consult Max Gluckman's study of the Barotse,[8] in which he shows how the norm of "the reasonable man" is used in cross-examination. I think any litigator who reads Gluckman will readily acknowledge that the Barotse are worthy colleagues in the art of cross-examination.) At any rate, the story is about young men and fire, and Maclean first tells us what sort of young men they were; then, he tells us about fire. I have already summarized Maclean's description of the basic distinctions between a ground fire, a crown fire, and a blow-up. I will only add that Maclean would have us acknowledge two matters. First, in order to understand fire, we need knowledge, organized into a science, so far as we are able to do so. But second, we should have no illusions about our ability to control fire; the human will is not always triumphant when it confronts nature.

I hope my exposition has not made tedious that which is elegant, for I am convinced that reading Maclean can teach one more about storytelling than all of the theorizing past or future. Lawyers and judges who tell stories, which is to say, lawyers and judges, can learn much by contemplating how his foreshadowing of the end intensifies the beginning and how he establishes the context by weaving together the theme of youth—young men in

---

8. Max Gluckman, *The Judicial Process Among the Barotse of Northern Rhodesia* (Glencoe, Ill.: Free Press, 1955).

a young organization using a young technology. Their youth was the tragedy, both that they died so young and that the youthfulness of their enterprise was the primary cause of their death. Furthermore, I think one can learn much about artistry by noticing the skill with which he sketches out the two antagonists, the young men and the fire, giving us a picture of what sort of young men these were and what sort of fire this was.

Chapter 1 ends with a few pages on storytelling. Throughout the book, Maclean from time to time tells us something about storytelling, and in due course I shall summarize what he says, since we can learn much not merely from what he does, but from what he says about what he does. This first statement is not his final statement, and so one should not give it more weight than it can bear. And indeed, it is somewhat opaque and mysterious. But let me quote:

> Although young men died like squirrels in Mann Gulch, the Mann Gulch fire should not end there, smoke drifting away and leaving terror without consolation of explanation, and controversy without lasting settlement. . . . This is a catastrophe that we hope will not end where it began; it might go on and become a story. It will not have to be made up—that is all important to us—but we do have to know in what odd places to look for missing parts of the story about a wildfire and of course have to know a story and a wildfire when we see one. So this story is a test of its own belief—that in this cockeyed world there are shapes and designs, if only we have some curiosity, training, and compassion and take care not to lie or be sentimental. It would be a start to a story if this catastrophe were found to have circled around out there somewhere until it could return to itself with explanations of its own mysteries and with the grief it left behind, not removed, because grief has its own place at or near the end of things, but altered somewhat by the addition of something like wonder. . . . If we could say something like this . . . then what we would be talking about would start to change from catastrophe without a filled-in story to what could be called the story of a tragedy, but tragedy would be only a part of it, as it is of life. (*Young Men and Fire*, 37–38)

As I have said, the passage will not yield all we might wish to find on first reading, and we shall have to learn more from Maclean's later statements about storytelling. But I think it already clear that my use of Burke's pentad has only scratched the surface. Although the passage is opaque, it is clear enough already that not just any manipulation of the Burkean ratios can make a story, or at least, not according to Maclean. Maclean makes clear that a story must have the right sort of shape, although he does not yet make clear what sort of shape he will seek. Furthermore, he also makes it clear that a story will give us a particular sort of knowledge, even though he is not yet clear exactly what kind of knowledge that is.

In chapter 2 of part 1, Maclean takes us on a trip from the home base to the drop zone. He gives us more chronology, more detail, more information about the geology of the area and the organization of which the smoke jumpers were members. The jumpers are on the ground by 4:10 P.M. on August 5; by the time they organize their gear and get themselves ready to start out toward the fire it is 5:00 and eleven of them have less than an hour to live; two more, less than a day. So ends chapter 2. Chapter 2 is economical and elegant throughout; however, there is one passage especially worth our notice, since it adds to our understanding of what Maclean means by a story. The passage occurs as Maclean is discussing the geology of the Missouri River. He notes the massive cliffs on each side of the river and observes that the geologists tell us that once these cliffs were joined by massive stone arches. Consequently, as one boats the river and looks up, one sees sky where earlier there had been stone arches. These missing arches become a metaphor that Maclean uses to tell us something else about storytelling.

> Looking up, [one] can see that an arch, now disappeared into sky, originally joined both cliffs. There are also missing parts to the story of the lonely crosses ahead of us, almost invisible in deep grass near the top of a mountain. What if, by searching the earth and even the sky for these missing parts, we should find enough of them to see catastrophe change into the shape of remembered tragedy? Unless we are willing to escape into sentimentality or fantasy, often the best we can do with catastrophes, even our own, is to find out exactly what happened and restore some of the missing parts—hopefully, even the arch to the sky. (46–47)

Maclean here makes explicit what was probably already clear enough anyway, which is, that the storyteller must search out the missing parts and fill in the gaps. Sentimentality and fantasy are judged to be inadequate; we must seek out the truth.

In chapter 3, Maclean puts us on the ground, walking in. We go with the group down the gulch, the fire grows, they run, Dodge lights the escape fire. And chapter 3 ends, stopping the disaster just before death hits. As an exemplar of storytelling, one can note the skill here in knowing exactly when to stop and digress. In the story of the Mann Gulch fire, as in most stories, things are happening in more than one place. At the same time the sixteen are going down the gulch, people are acting elsewhere, and they too are connected to the story. So how does one connect them? Maclean uses chronology. At the very moment that Wag Dodge was leading his crew down the gulch, Robert Jansson was walking into the gulch from the bottom. The switch in chapter 4 to Jansson is dramatically effective since it shows the isolation of the smoke jumpers. There is no link between what Jansson is doing and what the sixteen are doing, which intensifies their isolation. The story of Jansson also heightens tension in another extraordinary way; he survived, they didn't. As Jansson walks in, he walks into the blow-up, yet he survives, presumably because the fire was blowing away from him up the gulch and not down it. Even so, he lost consciousness. He may be the only man who ever walked into a blow-up and lived to describe what it was like. Those further up the gulch were not so lucky.

In chapter 5, we return to Wag Dodge setting his escape fire, and Maclean tells us about the desperate last minutes. As he presents it, we get the contradictions in the testimony, the confusion, the incompleteness. Any experienced trial lawyer can sympathize with this storyteller's plight. In times of stress, people do not always observe well, and when I was a young trial lawyer, I was taught by my elders that there would be as many versions of an event as there were witnesses. Maclean acknowledges this problem, but he passes it by lightly, for he is interested in a deeper problem. Even given all of the contradictions, the testimony is radically incomplete. We have testimony from only three, Wag Dodge, who survived in the escape fire, and Robert Sallee and Walter Rumsey, who were somehow athletic enough to have outrun the fire to the top of the hill, and who were somehow lucky in a choice they made—they ran straight uphill, instead of trying to angle up the hill; it is harder to run straight up. There were two who survived the day, William Hellman and Joseph Sylvia, but died the next. We know more about their movements than we do about the others who died, but not enough. Maclean characterizes the thirteen as "the missing persons in this story." And he uses the occasion to stake out boldly his own ambition as a storyteller. He starts by explaining why they are missing persons in the story as so far told and tells us what he intends to do about it.

There is a simple aspect of historiography, of course, to explain why, after last seen by the living, they pass silently out of the story and their own tragedy until their tragedy is over and they are found as bodies: no one who lived saw their sufferings. The historian, for a variety of reasons, can limit his account to first hand witnesses, although a shortage of first hand witnesses probably does not explain completely why contemporary accounts of the Mann Gulch fire avert their eyes from the tragedy. If a storyteller thinks enough of storytelling to regard it as a calling, unlike a historian he cannot turn from the suffering of his characters. A storyteller, unlike a historian, must follow compassion wherever it leads him. He must be able to accompany his characters, even into smoke and fire, and bear witness to what they thought and felt even when they themselves no longer knew. This story of the Mann Gulch fire will not end until it feels able to walk the final distance to the crosses with those who for the time being are blotted out by smoke. They were young and did not leave much behind them and need someone to remember them. (101–2)

At trial, we too must sometimes tell the story of that for which there are no witnesses, and there are times when we might be strong enough to tell it with compassion.

Although Dodge survived because he set the escape fire, his acts caused a controversy. Those whose sons had died asked a question that anyone would naturally ask: Did their sons die because of Dodge's fire? Were they burned by the main fire, or by the flames that Dodge set? Alternatively, did Dodge's escape fire cut off the route they might have followed, trap them lower down on the mountain, and make it inevitable that they died? For the law, these questions would be primary. Maclean intends to answer them, but they are not his primary question, and so he sets them aside for the moment.

The controversial history that was soon to follow and has lasted ever since charges that Dodge's escape fire, set in front of the main fire, was the fire that actually burned some of the crew and cut off others from escaping. Historical questions the storyteller must face, although in a place of his own choosing, but his most immediate question as he faces new material is always, Will anything strange or wonderful happen here? The rights and wrongs come later and likewise the scientific know-how.

The most strange and wonderful thing on the hillside as the escape fire swept up it, shutting it out of sight in smoke and heat, is that a spot of it remained cool. The one cool spot was inside Dodge. (102–3)

Since Maclean has discovered something "strange and wonderful," he breaks off the chronology of his story and pursues the mystery of the "cool spot." He gives us more of about Dodge's character and his invention, which was perhaps the reinvention of lost knowledge. There were precedents for escape fires, but there is no reason to believe that Dodge knew of them. Indeed, one should not exaggerate the similarities between Dodge's use of an escape fire and the precedents. Maclean summarizes as follows:

Of course, Dodge had a Smokejumper's knowledge that if you can't reach the top of the hill you should turn and try to work back through burned-out areas in the front of a fire. But with flames of the fire front solid and hundred yards deep he had to invent the notion that he could burn a hole in the fire. Perhaps, though, his biggest invention was not to burn a hole in the fire but to lie down in it. Perhaps all he could patent about his invention was the courage to lie down in his fire. Like a lot of inventions, it could be crazy and consume the inventor. His invention, taking as much guts as logic, suffered the immediate fate of many other inventions—it was thought to be crazy by those who first saw it. Somebody said, "To hell with that," and they kept going, most of them to their deaths. (106)

Maclean does a quick flash-forward at this point, and tells us about Dodge's death. He was soon discovered to be suffering from Hodgkin's disease, and died within five years of the Mann Gulch fire.

His wife knew when he entered the hospital for the last time that he knew it was for the last time. Like many woodsmen, he always carried a jackknife with him in his pants pocket, always. She told me that when he entered the hospital for the last time he left his jackknife home on his bedroom table, so he and she knew. (106)

Chapter 6 is the story of the failed rescue attempts, that is, of how the outside world first learned of the tragedy (Dodge and Sallee walked out), how the crew walked in to where Rumsey was caring for Hellman, how they carried Hellman and Sylvia out, and how Hellman and Sylvia died. Since Maclean can write so well, the futility of the attempt is given great dignity. The chapter also becomes a story of Jansson, who was in charge of the rescue squad, and so Maclean again breaks chronology and shows us some of the cost of Jansson's surviving. Since he survived, he became obsessed with trying to understand and he returned again and again to the site pacing, measuring, and observing. He tormented himself, and he finally had to separate himself from the place.

> In the end, he had to rescue himself from Mann Gulch by asking to be transferred to another ranger district. It had got so that he could not sleep at night, remembering the smell of it, and his dog would no longer come in but cried all night outside, knowing that something had gone wrong with him. (123)

Having flashed forward to events after the fire in the lives of Wag Dodge and Robert Jansson, Maclean ends part 1 with chapter 7, a story about Harry Gisborne. Gisborne is described as "the man above all others who made the study of fire a science" (124). This high praise rests not merely on his substantive achievements, his own careful investigations, but also his creation of a core of disciples in the Forest Service who advanced his cause, the use of science in the study of fire. Robert Jansson was one of Harry Gisborne's disciples. Despite his illness, Gisborne made the trip to Mann Gulch (without informing his doctor) to examine the evidence on the ground before winter destroyed it. Gisborne had a theory about the causes of a blow-up, a complicated theory about the interrelationships of mountains and winds; part of his theory was that the vortex of a fire would always rotate clockwise. He persuaded his disciple, Jansson, to accompany him.

The plan was for them to stop every hundred yards and rest; with all of these stops, what would have been a half-hour walk took two hours. Jansson took notes about their conversation at each rest stop, and these notes reveal that by stop fifteen, Gisborne had decided his theories were wrong. Having decided that all of his theories about a blow-up were incorrect, Gisborne began to doubt that there had even been a blow-up. The evidence on the ground did not persuade him, and so by stop twenty-eight, he declared to Jansson that there had never been a blow-up. But at stop thirty-two Jansson pointed out the evidence, Gisborne changed his mind, and became enthusiastic about the prospects of a new theory. He wanted to proceed immediately to investigate, but Jansson insisted they return. On the way back at stop thirty-five, Jansson records Gisborne as saying, "I'm glad I got a chance to get up here. Tomorrow we can get all our dope together and work on Hypothesis Number One. Maybe it will lead to a theory" (138). At stop thirty-seven, he died.

The unstated parallel of Maclean's own inquiry to Gisborne's makes this ending especially moving. Maclean offers the following as Gisborne's epitaph, and I read it as also his own. Maclean would go further in finding an answer than Gisborne was able to, but he too died with his inquiry unfinished. Maclean describes Gisborne's death as follows:

> For a scientist, this is a good way to live and die, maybe the ideal way for any of us—excitedly finding we were wrong and excitedly waiting for tomorrow to come so we can start over again, get our new dope together, and find a Hypothesis Number One all over again. And being basically on the right track when we were wrong. (139)

This ends part 1 of the book, and I am not ashamed to admit that my taking of notes was not always efficient, since more than once my sight was blurred. Part 1 tells the basic story, but there are gaps, and in part 2, Maclean attempts to learn more. He begins chapter 8 as follows: "We enter now a different time zone, even a different world of time. Suddenly comes the world of slow-time. . ." (143). If there was ever a fitting metaphor for a trial, for an inquiry after the fact, "slow-time" is it.

As Maclean begins this new phase of his book, he reflects once again on this enterprise of telling true stories. He states:

> There may somewhere be an ending to this story, although it might take a storyteller's faith to proceed on a quest to find it and on the way to retain the belief that it might both be true and fit together dramatically. A story that honors the dead realistically partly atones for their sufferings, and so instead of leaving us in moral bewilderment, adds dimensions to our acuteness in watching the universe . . . at work. (144)

This short paragraph contains an important clue about storytelling, which is, a clue about our need for stories, about what stories can give us—a story "adds dimensions to our acuteness." In short, we see better if we read better.

This short paragraph is followed by a long paragraph I confess I find knotted and difficult. If I interpret it correctly, it is a commentary on the "storyteller's faith" that the story "might both be true and fit together dramatically." He seems to find part of the truth of a story in the relationship between story and memory; we remember life as a set of fragmentary stories (and herein Maclean also seems to imply that we become what we remember). He also complicates the concept of dramatic form by asserting that a good story must honor the id, the disorderly, and also the counterimpulse of the ego, since the id is part of life, and the counterimpulse toward order is an impulse toward sanity. But let me quote, so that one can judge for oneself:

> True, though, it [the story] must be. Far back in the impulses to find this story is a storyteller's belief that at times life takes on the shape of art and that the remembered remnants of these moments are largely what we come to mean by life. The short semihumorous comedies we live, our long certain tragedies, and our springtime lyrics and limericks make up most of what we are. They become almost all of what we remember of ourselves. Although it would be too fancy to take these moments of our lives that seemingly have shape and design as proof we are inhabited by an impulse to art, yet deep within us is a counterimpulse to the id or whatever name is presently attached to the disorderly, the violent, the catastrophic both in and outside us. As a feeling, this counterimpulse to the id is a kind of craving for sanity, for things belonging to each other, and results in a comfortable feeling when the universe is seen to take a garment from the rack that seems to fit. Of course, both impulses need to be present to explain our lives and our art, and probably go a long way to explain why tragedy, inflamed with the disorderly, is generally regarded as the most composed art form. (144–45)

The balance of this opening chapter is a quick survey of the previous inquiries into the Mann Gulch fire. The Forest Service conducted an administrative inquiry; a lawsuit was filed; there was a movie. Those of us who have lived long enough to have learned certain things about the world can know in advance that all three were unsatisfactory. Maclean's account confirms and does not refute our weary expectations. The Forest Service inquiry failed because those who convened it had an agenda that was far removed from Maclean's agenda to find some unity between truth and art. Theirs was far simpler—to disclaim fault in the face of public outcry. The inquiry was too hastily done, and after the fact, the records scattered and misfiled. The lawsuit was unsatisfactory because it never addressed the merits of the case. It was held that the representatives of the deceased were entitled to no more than the statutory death benefit. They were not permitted to charge and prove fault, since the government cannot be sued as an ordinary person can be. In short, technical questions of jurisdiction and statutory interpretation cut the legal inquiry short, which in truth seems to be the norm for legal inquiry. In all cases, decisions must be made under constraints of jurisdiction and procedure, which become in turn barriers to finding a unity between truth and art. The movie, of course, romanticized the event. In the movie, there is a second fire after the first fire, and once again the foreman lights an escape fire, but this time the crew heeds him "and everybody lives happily ever after" (155). Only a few eccentrics suppose that one can go to the movies and see reality; most of the audience want their movies to be an escape from the reality of their life, and those who make movies understand this. So this movie, like all movies, romanticized.

But Maclean has higher standards, and he sets out to tell a story that will unite truth and art. In doing so, he becomes friends with some truly fine people who work for the Forest Service, and so he ends this chapter with a tribute to them. One should remember, and Maclean is right in reminding us of this fact, that one of the satisfactions of inquiry is the friends one makes while pursuing it. Those who help someone who wants to learn may be hard to find but they are good to know.

Part 2 is an acute description of conducting an inquiry. Since investigation is not the topic of this book, I shall pass by it lightly. Maclean first starts with the evidence of the site, with what one can see on the ground if one knows how to look. Our knowledge of police work elsewhere confirms the wisdom of this technique. The scene of the crime, the crumpled remains of an aircraft, the debris left by a bomb, are the best evidence, and a careful sifting will reveal more clues and generate more hypotheses than any other source of information. Maclean even sought out the two survivors, Sallee and Rumsey, and walked with them back across the site. With the witnesses, Maclean located the crevice in the rock through which they escaped and the exact spot at which Wag Dodge set his fire.

A good investigator must also know when to abandon an idea. One cannot conduct an investigation without having hypotheses to investigate, but the real risk is that a hypothesis about how something happened may harden too soon. Maclean describes this problem with humor in two golden sentences.

Coming to recognize you are wrong is like coming to recognize you are sick. You feel bad long before you admit you have any of the symptoms and certainly long before you are willing to take your medicine. (189)

But Maclean in fact determined that his witnesses had reconstructed their movements incorrectly, and he drew up a new strategy of inquiry and revisited the site. As Maclean reflects on how the mistakes were made, he notes two things. The very direction from which they had approached the site predisposed them to error, for they had come on the scene from the wrong angle. And he also reflected on how tricky the human memory is. Sallee and Rumsey had remembered with great clarity and accuracy what had happened after they were safe. Once they had made it across the ridge, incidental details were precisely identified. But before that, the desperate moments of their attempt to survive had killed memory. The effort of surviving had so focused their attention that all details were lost.

Maclean also understands that any investigator must learn how to assimilate scientific knowledge in realms far from his expertise. He mapped out the site as carefully as possible, measuring the distances that the young men must have traveled, never forgetting that all of his measurements were only estimates. He sought out the experts in the science of fire and let them teach him the theory and the physics of how a fire spreads and blows up. And finally he gave his experts the best factual probabilities that he had been able to develop so that they could use mathematical models to track out the relative movements of the fire and the men. This mathematical analysis is summarized in a graph (269) and then the graph is translated into a narrative (270–77), in which the unequal race of young men with fire is given mathematical inevitability, and in Maclean's telling, mathematics is poetics.

The conclusion of part 2 is Maclean's reassessment of what one might call the "legal" issue, that is, did the escape fire make it impossible for any of the crew to get to the top of the ridge. The main fire was burning up the gulch, from west to east, and if the escape fire burned in that direction it might well have made it more difficult for those downhill of it to go north up to the top of the ridge. However, Sallee and Rumsey testified that the escape fire had burned north up the ridge and not east up the gulch. If their testimony is correct, then the escape fire did not cut off the rest of the crew and prevent them from angling toward the top of the ridge. If they are right, it was the speed of the main fire that did them in. The "legal question" thus reduces itself to a more precise question, which is, how could the two fires move at right angles to each other? The explanation rests on understanding a convection effect, which Maclean explains with elegance. A whirlwind of fire can create a windless zone immediately in front of it. An escape fire in this windless zone could burn straight uphill until it intersected the main fire. This is only probable, not certain, but it is a probability consistent with all of the evidence and which unites testimony with physics.

We turn now to part 3, in which Maclean asks what the fire was like and what it was like for the young men who fled it. As I read, I was curious to know whether and how part 3 had been informed by what Maclean had learned in his inquiry. What had part 2 given part 1 to make part 3 possible? Maclean has indeed filled in some of the gaps in the story. He knows more about the physics of fire and about why a blow-up does what it does. He also knows more about the precise path traced out by those who lost their race with fire. Indeed, his knowledge has now progressed to where he can map out on the ground (with probability as the standard of accuracy) the relative movement of the fire and the men.

But how does this increasing accuracy in the detail enable him to do what he most wants to do, which is to witness their suffering and give a voice to it? The answer, I think, is that the detail is necessary, but not sufficient. The detail is necessary because it gives factual specificity to such questions as how far they moved and how quickly they did it. With the detail, he can trace out in his mind a vivid picture of their movements that was otherwise impossible. Without the detail, those who died are absent, just as they were in part 1, but with the detail, the imagination can go to work because the imagination then has an image to work on. To see in the mind's eye is perhaps more important than our educational system acknowledges, and Antonio de Nicolas and David R. Lachterman may well be right when they say that we need to recover the ancient understanding of the philosophical importance of the image.[9] But even if constructing an image of details has no general philosophical significance, it is important to the storyteller.[10] In

9. See Antonio T. deNicolas, *Powers of Imagining* (Albany: State University of New York Press, 1986), and David R. Lachterman, *The Ethics of Geometry: A Genealogy of Modernity* (New York: Routledge, 1989).

10. See Peter Elbow, *Writing with Power* (New York: Oxford University Press, 1981), 322–23: "I can illustrate the process [of vision] most vividly with a workshop game where you try to tell images so that others actually see them. What often happens is that the student describes something, perhaps a maple tree in the middle of the front lawn with flowers growing around the trunk. But it doesn't quite work. It doesn't make me *see* it, I say, 'Wait. I can't see it. You must not have seen it. Close your eyes and wait till you really see it. Stop looking for words, look for the vision itself.

order for Maclean to do what he wishes to do, he needs to use his storyteller's imagination and imagine what it would be like to run that route, on that hillside, under those conditions. His story of the final moments of those who died has no greater proof than its performance; it has the authority of art (*Young Men and Fire*, 296–300).

In the intense heat, each was alone. Since fire had consumed all the oxygen they suffocated, which medical evidence tells us is one of the less painful ways to die. By the time they burned, they were already dead. But death was also sudden, since young men like them feel themselves to be unconquerable. From the threat of sudden death, the Book of Common Prayer pleads, "Good Lord, deliver us," and Maclean cites this venerable source for one of the thoughts they must have had. Since death was sudden, whatever thoughts there were would have been short. Fear most likely was burned away, leaving only self-pity and bewilderment. We have the testimony of Sallee and Rumsey, whose memory is also imperfect, that something like this would have been thought.

> The two living survivors of the Mann Gulch fire have told me that, as they went up the last hillside, they remember thinking only, "My God, how could you do this to me? I cannot be allowed to die so young and so close to the top!" They said they could remember hearing their voices saying this out loud. (299)

Discerning what they thought requires one to step along with them in the imagination. As for what they did, there is better evidence.

> Although we can enter their last thoughts and feelings only by indirection, we are sure of the final act of many of them. Doctor Hawkins, the physician who went in with the rescue crew the night the men were burned, told me that, after the bodies had fallen, most of them had risen again, taken a few steps, and fallen again, this

---

Don't hurry.' And we wait a bit while the speaker closes her eyes and tries to see the image clearly, and then she says, 'I can see it now, but it's a little bit different now.' And she tells her image, but the tree isn't in the middle of the lawn. It's really near the sidewalk. And it doesn't have flowers around it, it has long strands of scraggly grass that the lawnmower didn't get. And as she tells it, it *does* work, we all see it clearly. It's as though her first image was an imperfect or distorted view of the 'real' image, the second one. The first time she was trying to see it through a poor telescope so she had to invent some details. When I push, she focuses the lens better and can finally see the image clearly."

final time like pilgrims in prayer, facing the top of the hill, which on that slope is nearly east. Ranger Jansson, in charge of the rescue crew, independently made the same observation.

The evidence, then, is that at the very end beyond thought and beyond fear and beyond even self-compassion and divine bewilderment there remains some firm intention to continue doing for ever and ever what we last hoped to do on earth. By this final act they had come about as close as body and spirit can to establishing a unity of themselves with earth, fire, and perhaps the sky. (299–300)

IV

I fear that some who have read this far may be disappointed that I end with Maclean. I have said why the fictions of *Marbury* and *McCulloch* are unsatisfactory, but all I have offered by way of a positive recommendation is a single example, a story of death by fire. To one who might be disappointed, I ask, "Why are you disappointed? Do you want a *theory* that distinguishes good stories from bad?"

Recall that in the introduction I discussed the difficulty of theory. I admire good theories, just as Maclean does, but one honors good theories by not accepting bad ones, and a theory is bound to be bad if it is built on the wrong sort of objects. In the introduction, I used Chomsky to argue that topics such as "persuasion" or "communication" or "language" do not mark out a proper theoretical object. Chomsky has focused on the right sort of object—our biological capacity to understand language—because the topic of language as a whole is too rich and too open-ended to permit good theories. By analogy, I judge that the topic of storytelling in law is likewise not the sort of practice about which there can be a theory.

However, this last paragraph may be too abstract, so perhaps I should be more personal. I have been teaching law for some time now, and I have an observation about the legal academy: law students want rules; law professors want theories. This desire for rules and theories is passionately felt, and perhaps Jerome Frank was right to ground this desire for certainty in the superego,[11] and perhaps Gretchen Craft is right that dread and fear of the future is the fundamental motive driving judges, lawyers, and those who

---

11. Jerome Frank, *Law and the Modern Mind* (New York: Brentano's, 1930).

study and teach the law.[12] But aside from the psychology of desire, there is also the aesthetics of explanation. I prefer to tell a story about storytelling. If it is true that storytelling is one of the fundamental ways to understand the world, then a good story does not need to be replaced by a good theory; a good story can stand on its own, and so I tell a story about Maclean's story. Since we can use stories to think about the world—a good story "adds dimensions to our acuteness in watching the universe . . . at work"—I have tried to use Maclean's story to think about legal stories, but all are free to puzzle as they wish.

Are there lessons, then, that we can learn from Maclean? Let it be granted that lawyers and judges will continue to tell fictional stories about constitutional law. What does Maclean have to teach us about how to make these stories better? Maclean's ambition was to discover a true story about the Mann Gulch fire, and we can share that ambition; we want to tell the truest possible story about constitutional law. But as his book makes clear, discovering a truth that might take on the shape of a story requires a skill, an art, that does not come easily, and perhaps the most important quality we need to bring to the inquiry is the right sort of imagination. As Maclean says:

> We do have to know in what odd places to look for missing parts of the story about a wildfire [or a constitution] and of course we have to know a story [and a constitution] when we see one. So this story is a test of its own belief—that in this cockeyed world there are shapes and designs, if only we have some curiosity, training, and compassion and take care not to lie or be sentimental.

Maclean's advice is not a list of disconnected items—know where to look, know what you are looking for, don't lie, don't be sentimental. The several injunctions reflect a single vision of imaginative fullness and completeness. As Maclean shows, a storyteller must persist in the inquiry until the story is complete and full. Unfortunately, we are tempted to tell sentimental tales (the path of the law has been onward and upward), and thus lie, because we weaken and give up before we look in all the places we should look. Sometimes we weaken because we are afraid to look; we may cling to a sentimental tale about the path of the law so tightly that we are unwilling to look. And sometimes we are weak simply because we are ignorant—we

---

12. Gretchen Craft, "The Persistence of Dread in Law and Literature," 102 *Yale L. J.* 521 (1992).

don't know where to look. When we are ignorant, we may become disoriented and then desperately adopt some sentimental lie to give us ease.

John Keats's praise of Shakespeare offers an astringent tonic against the sentimental impulse: "And it at once struck me what quality went to form a Man of Achievement, especially in Literature, and which Shakespeare possessed so enormously—I mean *Negative Capability*, that is, when a man is capable of being in uncertainties, mysteries, doubts without any irritable reaching after fact and reason."[13]

I understand Keats's praise of Shakespeare as Walter Jackson Bate has interpreted it; we should emphasize the word "irritable."[14] If we follow Bate, we can interpret Keats's praise as a warning that we should not fear mystery as much as we do and that we should not dissolve mystery and doubt by an "irritable reaching" for some *single* fact or reason that we designate as *the* fact or *the* reason.

Lawyers and judges are under an enormous pressure to reach for some single fact or reason—the pressure to assign blame. In the Mann Gulch fire, this temptation was also present. Recall the controversy over Wag Dodge's escape fire: Did it cut off an escape route? Did it cause the death of thirteen young men? But recall also that Maclean refused to accept this controversy as his primary topic:

> Historical questions [about causation and fault] the storyteller must face, although in a place of his own choosing, but his most immediate question as he faces new material is always, Will anything strange or wonderful happen here? The rights and wrongs come later and likewise the scientific know-how. (*Young Men and Fire*, 102)[15]

It would be easy, but I think wrong, for lawyers to suppose that Maclean's priority is fine for him, but not for them. Lawyers (and legal academics) might indulge Maclean, but ignore his principles, by asserting: "One can understand that a storyteller might give the place of honor to whatever is 'strange or wonderful,' but that is the wrong priority for us. We can't follow that advice. With us, the 'rights and wrongs' and the 'scientific know-how' must come first." This sort of response is understandable, but suspect.

---

13. Letter to George and Thomas Keats, December 22, 1817.
14. Walter Jackson Bate, *John Keats* (Cambridge: Harvard University Press, Belknap Press, 1963), 249.
15. Compare Maclean's comments on the "storyteller" with Keats's on Shakespeare. They are saying the same thing.

Let me respond to the lawyerly sense of priority with a lawyerly cite to precedent. "Knowledge is essential to understanding; and understanding should precede judging."[16] Justice Brandeis is right; it is foolish to judge the "rights and wrongs" before one understands. To be sure, Brandeis himself sought understanding in statistics, whereas Maclean would begin with asking whether there is "anything strange or wonderful." There need be no opposition. Like Brandeis, Maclean honors the virtues of statistics (he presented the statistical case for believing that smoke jumpers had helped reduce the number of massive forest fires) and science (he studied the physics of fire, and how a fire explodes into a blow-up). Indeed, Maclean even calculated (with the aid of experts) the details of time and distance in order to encode the race between fire and young men in mathematics.

Yet even so, although there need be no opposition, still there is a distinction, which perhaps I can sneak up on by asking, Why does one ever want to know about "the rights and wrongs"? Why does one want to have "the scientific know-how"? For most of us, the answer is simple enough—it's my job. But if the job has some value beyond wages (currency or status), perhaps the value lies in understanding something "strange or wonderful." The mysteries are both the start and the end of our inquiry. We start our inquiry because there is some mystery or puzzle that provokes us, and in the end, we hope to be able to look at the mystery straight on, to see it clearly. As Maclean says:

> There may somewhere be an ending to this story, although it might take a storyteller's faith to proceed on a quest to find it and on the way to retain the belief that it might both be true and fit together dramatically. A story that honors the dead realistically partly atones for their sufferings, and so instead of leaving us in moral bewilderment, adds dimensions to our acuteness in watching the universe . . . at work. (*Young Men and Fire*, 144).

Consequently, when Wag Dodge sets his escape fire, Maclean turns aside from "the rights and wrongs" and looks for that which is "strange or wonderful": "The most strange and wonderful thing on the hillside as the escape fire swept up it, shutting it out of sight in smoke and heat, is that a spot of it remained cool. The one cool spot was inside Dodge" (103).

16. Louis D. Brandeis, *Jay Burns Baking Co. v. Bryan*, 264 21 Sup. Ct. 504 at 520 (1924), dissenting opinion.

So too, Maclean ends his book with a mystery, the final act of those who suffered and died. Their final act was that they fell, then rose, took a few steps, then fell again.

> The evidence, then, is that at the very end beyond thought and beyond fear and beyond even self-compassion and divine bewilderment there remains some firm intention to continue doing for ever and ever what we last hoped to do on earth. By this final act they had come about as close as body and spirit can to establishing a unity of themselves with earth, fire, and perhaps the sky. (300)

These passages from Maclean may not persuade you that lawyers (whether they be academic or nonacademic) should be willing to set aside their inquiry after "the rights and wrongs" and for "scientific know-how" and look first to discover what is "strange or wonderful." You may not be persuaded because I have not offered any theory that entails the priority. My only authority is Maclean's performance. If a story is good enough authority, then Maclean's story will be good enough; if not, not. But let me suppose that one is willing to try to be the sort of storyteller that Maclean has tried to be, at least to the extent of conducting a temporary experiment. If one were to try out this experience, how might storytelling in constitutional law be different?

Suppose we looked at *Marbury* and *McCulloch* and asked: Did anything strange and wonderful happen here? *Marbury* is the first step in bringing together the constitution and the law so that we can begin to have something known as constitutional law. Although the language spoken in *Marbury* is the language of dichotomies, of limits, the achievement of the decision is something far more complex. The limits that Marshall scribed out between the legislature, the executive, and the judiciary need not be seen as walls or fences that constitute "No Trespassing" signs; instead, they can be seen as a first attempt to construct a division of labor. Each department needs a primary role so that each can cooperate with the other. As Justice Jackson once said: "While the Constitution diffuses power the better to secure liberty, it also contemplates that practice will integrate the dispersed powers into a workable government. It enjoins upon its branches separateness but interdependence, autonomy but reciprocity."[17] Jackson's thesis that we are both separate and interdependent, that we should act both autonomously and

---

17. *Youngstown Sheet & Tube v. Sawyer*, 343 U.S. 579 at 635 (1952).

reciprocally, seems right. Milner Ball's *Lying Down Together*[18] tells stories about the law that attempt to apply this insight.

In *McCulloch*, Marshall spoke a language of growth that is false, but his achievement has proved to be far richer than that inept metaphor suggests. When we honor *McCulloch*, we need not be so foolish as to suppose that the Constitution today relates to the Constitution then as does a tree to a seed. Law does not grow from its antecedents as a tree grows from a root. Instead, we do something far more complex; we read John Marshall's opinions and use them as precedents. James Boyd White's *Justice as Translation*[19] tries to explain how our use of precedents can be understood as translating from then to now, as an uncertain process of finding a new language that can restate the old.

These experiments of White and Ball extend our imagination by revealing to us some part of what is "strange and wonderful." To be sure, we also need more stories and better stories about "rights and wrongs" and about "scientific knowledge." Each type of story has its own time and place, and I do not want to be understood as recommending that only one type of story be told. In fact, I recommend that we should each tell the story that we have the talent to tell. When we sit down to rest, the best any of us can hope for is that someone might say of us what Norman Maclean said of Harry Gisborne, that we were "basically on the right track when we were wrong" (*Young Men and Fire*, 139).

18. Milner S. Ball, *Lying Down Together: Law, Metaphor, and Theology* (Madison: University of Wisconsin Press, 1985).

19. James Boyd White, *Justice as Translation: An Essay in Cultural and Legal Criticism* (Chicago: University of Chicago Press, 1990).

Index